日本茅葺き紀行

Exploring Japanese Thatch

[一社] 日本茅葺き文化協会 ●編
Edited by Japan Thatching Cultural Association

安藤邦廣　上野弥智代 ●著
Kunihiro Ando and Yachiyo Ueno

杉原バーバラ ●訳
Translated by Barbara Sugihara

農文協

道祖神のワラ葺き（長野県池田町、2017）

目次
CONTENTS

茅葺きの里 16 マップ	Map of Thatched Villages	2
いま茅葺き、生きものたちとつながる風景を取り戻そう	Thatch Now to Restore Living Landscapes	4

《茅葺きの里　Thatched Villages》

アイヌのチセ	Ainu *Chise* (Hokkaido)	6
南部の曲家と芝棟	Nambu *Magariya* and *Shiba-mune*	12
秋田の中門造	Akita's *Chumon-zukuri*	18
田麦俣のタカハッポウ造	The *Takahappo-zukuri* of Tamugimata (Yamagata Pref.)	26
会津流の茅葺き	Aizu-Style Thatch (Fukushima Pref.)	34
筑波流の茅葺き	Tsukuba-Style Thatch (Ibaraki Pref.)	50
関東山地の甲屋根	The Helmet Roofs of the Kanto Mountains	64
北信州の茅葺き	Thatch in Northern Shinshu (Nagano Pref.)	80
五箇山の合掌造	Gokayama's *Gassho-zukuri* (Toyama Pref.)	92
白川郷の合掌造	The *Gassho-zukuri* of Shirakawa-go (Gifu Pref.)	102
美山町北集落	Kita Village in Miyama (Kyoto Pref.)	116
東播磨の茅葺き	The Thatched Houses of Higashi Harima (Hyogo Pref.)	124
出雲平野の反り棟	The Curved Roofs of the Izumo Plain (Shimane Pref.)	130
筑後川流域の杉皮葺き	Cedar-Bark Thatch in the Chikugo River Basin	138
佐賀のくど造	The *Kudo-zukuri* of Saga Pref.	144
九州、沖縄の分棟造と高倉	Divided-Roof Houses and Raised Storehouses in Kyushu and Okinawa	152

《茅葺き図鑑　Reference》

逆葺き	Reverse Thatching	24
茅場の多面的機能と炭素の循環	The Multifaceted Functions of *Kaya* Fields and the Carbon Cycle	32
北上川のヨシ原	*Yoshi* (Reed) Beds in the Kitakami River (Miyagi Pref.)	46
ヨシ原の多面的機能と炭素の循環	The Multifaceted Functions of Reed Beds and the Carbon Cycle	48
霞ヶ浦のヨシ原	The *Yoshi* (Reed) Beds of Lake Kasumigaura (Ibaraki Pref.)	62
富士山麓の茅場	The *Kaya* Fields at the Foot of Mt. Fuji (Shizuoka Pref.)	76
白馬山麓カリヤスの茅場	*Kariyasu* Fields at Mt. Hakuba (Nagano Pref.)	88
カリヤスの段階的利用	Stages in the Utilization of *Kariyasu*	100
琵琶湖のヨシ原	The *Yoshi* (Reed) Beds of Lake Biwa (Shiga Pref.)	112
四国の茶堂	Shikoku's Tea Pavilions	136
阿蘇の茅場	The *Kaya* Fields at Mt. Aso (Kumamoto Pref.)	150

《茅葺きの技　Techniques》

茅葺きの材料	Thatching Materials	170
茅葺きの道具	Thatching Tools	172
茅葺きの棟仕舞	Ridge Finishings	174

作図（pp2-3,32-33,48-49,100-101,172）　伊藤梨沙
Illustrations on pp. 2-3, 32-33, 48-49, 100-101, 172 by Risa Ito

9. 五箇山の合掌造
Gokayama's *Gassho-zukuri* (Toyama Pref.)

3. 秋田の中門造
Akita's *Chumon-zukuri*

4. 田麦俣のタカハッポウ造
The *Takahappo-zukuri* of Tamugimata (Yamagata Pref.)

10. 白川郷の合掌造
The *Gassho-zukuri* of Shirakawa-go (Gifu Pref.)

13. 出雲平野の反り棟
The Curved Roofs of the Izumo Plain (Shimane Pref.)

14. 筑後川流域の杉皮葺き
Cedar Bark Thatch in the Chikugo River Basin

15. 佐賀のくど造
The *Kudo-zukuri* of Saga Pref.

16. 九州、沖縄の分棟造と高倉
Divided-Roof Houses and Raised Storehouses in Kyushu and Okinawa

12. 東播磨の茅葺き
The Thatched Houses of Hig Harima (Hyogo

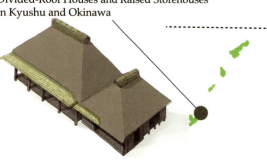

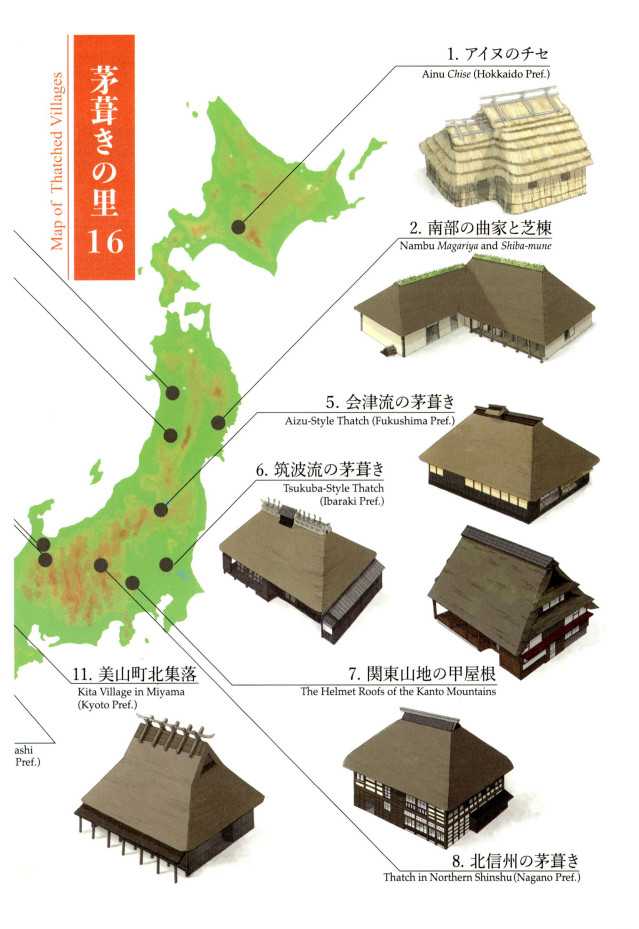

いま茅葺き、生きものたちとつながる風景を取り戻そう

日本茅葺き文化協会代表理事　筑波大学名誉教授　安藤邦廣

北海道から沖縄諸島まで南北3000kmに渡る日本列島には、その多様な気候風土や地形に適応して、地域色豊かな茅葺き民家が発達している。

それは、稲作農業を基盤としながらも、その地域の独自の生業の中で、茅の資源を大切に使うように技術が工夫されたものでもある。

茅とは、屋根を葺く植物の総称であり、ススキ、ヨシなどのイネ科の多年草や笹、竹など地域によってさまざまな植物が選ばれてきた。また、小麦ワラや稲ワラなどのように穀物生産の過程で生じる殻も利用されてきた。

これらのイネ科の多年草は、毎年刈り取ることでその生育環境が維持され、再生産の持続可能な資源である。しかし温暖で多雨な日本では、茅刈りをやめると草原は森林に戻っていく。茅を刈ることではじめて茅場は維持されるのである。

茅として最もよく使われるのがススキであり、次いで低湿地ではヨシである。これらの茅は、屋根を葺く資材であるとともに、牛馬などの家畜の飼料や敷草、田畑の緑肥、さらにスダレや炭俵などさまざまな生活用具をつくる材料としても重要な資源であった。そのため農村では、周辺の里山に広大な茅場、草刈り場を確保して、そこでの茅刈りが農家の暮らしの基本的な作業であった。

まっすぐで良質な茅は屋根に、太くて長いものはスダレに、曲がったり折れたりしたものは牛馬の飼料や敷草として、用途に応じて無駄なく使われてきた。葺き替えのときに生じる傷んだ古茅は、全て田畑の肥料となり、また牛馬の飼料や敷草となったものも、有益な堆肥となった。このように農家で刈り取った茅は、さまざまな用途に使われるが、最終的に全て肥料として農業の持続的な生産を支えたのである。すなわち屋根を茅で葺くということは、農業の営みそのものであったといえる。

茅葺きはそもそも村人が共同で葺くかたちが基本であり、ユイと呼ばれる相互扶助のしくみが各地に見られた。軽くて扱いやすい茅は、誰でも運搬加工ができ、特別な道具がなくとも縄で結んでとめることで屋根は葺ける。一部が傷めば茅を差し込むことで修理も容易である。大きな屋根も互いに助け合えば葺くことも難しいことではなかった。このようなユイによる屋根葺きは、白川郷のように今日まで受け継がれてきた地域もある。その一方で、農家の生業が多様化して、養蚕や畜産などの副業が盛んになり、農村が経済的に豊かになると、屋根を葺く職人が現れる。茅葺き職人は、集落を越えて屋根を葺き、各地を渡り歩く出稼ぎ職人集団も生まれた。その中で職人同士の技術の交流や切磋琢磨が生まれて、茅葺きの技術は大きく向上した。茅葺き専用の道具も開発された。こうして畜産業を営むための曲家や中門造、屋根裏で養蚕をするための甲造などが、このような職人の高い技術によって創意工夫され、地域色豊かな茅葺き民家の花が開いたのである。

このような茅葺きも農業の近代化が進む中で、その時代を終える。

茅場や草原は、明治のはじめ頃には国土の30％を超していたが、今日ではその多くが失われ、わずか2〜3％に減少したと推定されている。20世紀初頭には、農村のほとんどが茅葺き民家であったが、戦後の近代化の中で急速に姿を消し、その数も往時の2〜3％に減少している。このように茅葺きは農家の屋根であり、農業の近代化とともに茅葺き屋根が失われたのは避けることのできない流れであった。農業と切り離して屋根だけのために茅を刈るのは効率が悪く、茅葺きは手間がかかるだけのものとなり、農家の重荷となって姿を消していった。

茅場や草原とともに茅葺きが姿を消すと、日本の農村や里山の環境に大きな変化が生じた。琵琶湖や霞ヶ浦などの日本を代表する湖では、ヨシを刈らなくなったために、ヨシ原は減少した。湖の水質汚染が進み、豊かな水生生物の環境も失われた。また、野山の草原の消失により、そこに生息する草原性の生物の多くも絶滅危惧種としてその存続が危惧されている。例えば、春の七草、秋の七草など、日本人が親しんできた植物は、全て茅を刈ることで維持されてきた草原に咲く草花である。また蝶やトンボなどの昆虫やそれを食する野鳥などもその棲家を失い、絶滅の危機にさらされている。近年、生物多様性の維持の観点からも、茅場、草原の環境としての価値が見直されているのである。

今日、茅葺きの民家が歴史的文化として見直され、観光資源としても注目され、その再生を望む声が高まっている。茅葺きが本来農業の営みそのものであったこと、そして里山の環境と一体となって美しい風景をつくってきたことを考えれば、その連携の中で、茅葺きの再生を目指すことが重要である。

古来より日本人は自然の恵みに生かされ、その持続が叶う暮らしを営んできた。その生きものたちとつながる風景、そして環境の時代の象徴として、茅葺きはよみがえる。

Thatch Now to Restore Living Landscapes

Kunihiro Ando

President, Japan Thatching Cultural Association, Professor Emeritus, University of Tsukuba

Throughout the 3,000 kilometers of the Japanese archipelago, thatched houses developed in response to a wide range of climatic and geographic conditions, giving them much local variation. Although rice production is basic, different areas have also developed other industries of their own and have devised skills and technologies to utilize *kaya* resources carefully.

Kaya is the generic term for the plants that are used to thatch roofs. Miscanthus, reed, and other perennial gramineous grasses, dwarf bamboo, and bamboo are among the varieties of plants that have been chosen as thatching material. Stems obtained in the course of producing grains like wheat and rice are also used.

These perennial gramineous grasses are sustainable resources that can be reproduced if their growth environment is maintained by annual harvesting. In Japan's warm, rainy climate, however, the grasslands return to forest if the *kaya* is no longer cut. The *kaya* fields can be maintained only by harvesting the *kaya*.

Miscanthus is the most commonly used *kaya*, followed by reed where there are wetlands. In addition to being thatching materials, they were valuable resources for a wide variety of uses, including feed and bedding for livestock and green manure for the fields. They were also important for making screens, bags for charcoal, and many other household items. Because of this, villages maintained large *kaya* fields and grasslands in the local hills, and harvesting *kaya* was a basic task of rural life.

Kaya was not wasted: Good, straight *kaya* was used on the roof, thick long *kaya* was woven into screens, and bent or snapped *kaya* became fodder or bedding for animals. When a roof was rethatched, the damaged *kaya* was all reused as fertilizer in the fields, and the *kaya* that was used for raising animals also became valuable compost. In this way, the *kaya* that farmers harvested was put to a variety of uses, but in the end it all became fertilizer to support sustainable agriculture. In short, thatching a roof with *kaya* was itself an agricultural job.

Originally thatching was a cooperative village task, and systems of mutual assistance, called *yui*, existed in many places. *Kaya* is lightweight and easy to handle, so anyone can carry and process it, and it can be tied to a roof with rope even without special tools. Partial roof damage can easily be repaired by inserting new *kaya*, and with mutual help, it was not difficult to thatch even a large roof. There are some places, like Shirakawa-go, where this system is still carried on. At the same time, farmers diversified their occupations, going into sericulture and animal husbandry as sidelines, which made rural villages wealthy, and specialized craftsmen appeared to thatch roofs. Thatchers went to other villages to thatch, and groups of thatchers who journeyed far and wide also developed. This led to exchange of techniques and to competition among thatchers, which greatly raised the level of thatching skills. Tools specifically for thatching also were developed. This high level of craftsmanship among thatchers led to the invention of the *magariya* and *chumon-zukuri* for animal husbandry and the helmet roofs for sericulture in the roof space, creating lovely thatched houses with local color.

The modernization of agriculture, however, ended the era of thatched houses. When the Meiji era began in 1868, *kaya* fields and grasslands covered more than 30% of the land, but most have been lost, and the current estimate is a mere 2~3%. At the start of the 20th century, most villages were thatched, but in the course of postwar modernization, the demise of the thatched farmhouse roof was inevitable, and the number of thatched houses declined to 2~3% of what it had been. Harvesting thatch only for the roof, divorced from agriculture, was inefficient, and thatching itself took too much work, so the thatched roofs became burdensome for farmers and disappeared.

When thatched roofs disappeared along with *kaya* fields and grasslands, the environment of Japan's rural villages and low hills changed drastically. Because reed was no longer cut in Biwa, Kasumigaura, and other of Japan's largest lakes, the reed beds in the lakes dwindled. The lake water became increasingly polluted, and aquatic animals and plants lost a rich environment. At the same time, because grasslands disappeared from the hills, many of the plants and animals that live in them are in danger of extinction and are listed for special protection. The seasonal plants long familiar to the Japanese people flowered in the hills because the *kaya* fields were cut. Butterflies, dragonflies, and other insects, as well as the birds and other wildlife that eat them, lost a place to live and are now endangered species. In recent years, the importance of *kaya* fields and grasslands is being reevaluated from the perspective of biodiversity.

At the same time, thatched houses are being rediscovered as part of Japan's historical and cultural heritage and are also drawing attention as resources to promote tourism, so many people are hoping for their revival. Considering that thatching was originally an agricultural endeavor, and that together with the environment of the surrounding hills, it created a beautiful landscape, it is important to strive for the revival of thatch in this context.

From ancient times the Japanese people survived on the bounty of nature and lived in a way that made it sustainable. Thatched houses will revive as part of a landscape connected with living things and as the symbol of an era concerned with environmental sustainability.

アイヌのチセ
Ainu *Chise* (Hokkaido)

アイヌのコタン（集落）の復原
萱野茂二風谷アイヌ資料館（北海道平取町、2008）
チセと高床の倉庫もヨシ葺き

Reconstructed Ainu village
Kayano Shigeru Nibutani Ainu Museum (Biratori-cho, Hokkaido, 2008)
This *chise* and the raised-floor storehouse are thatched with reed.

ヨシ葺きのチセ全景（北海道平取町、2014）
チセの入り口として前室（モセㇺ）が付くのが一般的

View of a reed-thatched *chise* (Biratori, Hokkaido, 2014)
The entrance to the *chise* usually has a front room (*mosemu*).

棟はヨシをへの字に被せて、丸太の千木で押さえて縫い付けて固定する
破風に小さな煙出しが付く

The reed is bent into an inverted V shape over the ridge, held down with crossed logs (*chigi*) and lashed in place.
The gable has a small smoke vent.

屋根内部
サスの上に棟木と中間に母屋を配置し、その上に垂木とさらに横垂木を重ねて下地をつくる

Underside of the roof
The ridgepole and purlins are arranged over the braces, and the rafters and horizontal laths over these.

ヨシを葺き残して窓をつくる　外側にはヨシズをかけて開閉を調節する
Window created by leaving a part unthatched　A reed mat is hung on the outside to adjust the aperture.

川べりに自生するクマ笹原 A field of bamboo grass growing along a river

アイヌのチセ

チセは、北海道の先住民族アイヌの言葉で家という意味である。

チセの前には必ずモセムという前室がつき、そこを通じてチセに入る。前室は、物置や風除室の役割を果たす。

アイヌの人が家を建てるときにいちばん大切なことは、近くにきれいな飲み水があることである。つまり、集落は川や湖のほとりに建てられた。

チセは、丸太を掘建て柱とし、梁をのせた素朴なつくりである。小屋組は、同じく細い丸太をサスに組んでつくる。それらの接合は全て木の繊維の縄でしっかりと結ばれる。

屋根の材料は、水辺に自生するヨシやほとりに生えるクマ笹を用いる。ヨシで葺く場合は、長いまま根元を外に向けた真葺きとし、厚さ30cm程度に重ねて細い丸太で押さえて下地に縫い付け、それを段状に葺き上げていく。

壁も同様にヨシ葺きである。下段は根元を地面に立てて、上段はその上に被せるように逆さにした茅束を押しあて、根元を軒先に押し込む。その中段をぶどうづるの皮で下地に編み付けて固定する。

笹で葺く場合は、葉先を外に向ける逆葺きとして、1束ずつオニョウニレの木の繊維の縄で下地にくくり付け、丁寧に葺き重ねていく。壁も同様に1束ずつ下地に編み付けて葺き上げる。その厚さ約20cm。

Ainu *Chise*

In the language of the Ainu, the indigenous people of Hokkaido, *chise* means "house."

A *chise* always has a front room called *mosemu*, which, in addition to being the entrance, serves as storage space and protection against the wind. When building a house, the Ainu place the utmost importance on having a supply of clean drinking water nearby, so villages are built on the shores of rivers and lakes.

The *chise* is a simple structure with round logs sunk in the ground for posts and beams laid over them. Thin logs are assembled as braces to form the roof truss. All joins are lashed tightly with wood-fiber rope. The roof is thatched using reed (*yoshi*) that grows in the water or bamboo grass (*kuma-zasa*) growing on the shores. When reed is used, it is laid on the roof uncut, root end facing outwards, to a thickness of about 30 centimeters and held down with thin logs that are tied to the frame. This is repeated in stepped layers to the ridge.

The walls are also thatched with reed. On the lower part, the roots are placed on the ground; this layer is covered with bunches of reed laid so the tops hang down and the roots are pushed into the eaves. Grape vine bark is woven across the middle to attach the thatch to the frame.

With bamboo grass, the thatch is laid on the roof with the tops hanging down (*saka-buki*) and attached to the truss a bunch at a time using rope of elm fiber, working upwards in carefully-made layers. The walls are also attached to the frame a bundle at a time to a thickness of about 20 centimeters.

笹葺きのチセ外観　川村カ子トアイヌ記念館（北海道旭川市、2014）
屋根も壁もクマ笹の逆葺き
表面に笹の葉が密生する

Chise thatched with bamboo grass (Kawamura Kaneto Aynu Museum, Asahikawa, Hokkaido, 2014)
The roof and walls are bamboo grass *saka-buki*.
The bamboo leaves are closely packed on the surface.

笹を葺き残して窓をつくり、窓台は笹の根元を揃えて細い丸太で押さえて縫い付ける

A window made by leaving part of the wall unthatched   The windowsill is created by evening the root ends of the bamboo, weighting them down with a thin log, and stitching this in place.

笹葺きの壁内部
細かく配置した壁下地の横木に笹が1束ずつ隙間なく木の繊維で編み付けてある

Interior of a bamboo grass wall
Using wood-fiber rope, the bamboo grass is attached a bunch at a time to closely-placed horizontal laths so that there is no space between the bunches.

前室（モセム）からチセ内部を見る

View of the *chise* interior from the front room (*mosemu*)

チセ内部
床は土間住まいで中央に囲炉裏がきってある
囲炉裏は調理と暖房を兼ねて年中火を絶やすことはない
その熱が土間に蓄熱され、一定の温度が保たれる
厚い笹葺きの断熱性とあわせて、厳しい寒さを凌ぐことができる

Chise interior
A hearth is cut into the center of the earthen floor.
Used for cooking and heat, the hearth fire never dies out. The earthen floor retains the heat, keeping the house temperature relatively even.
This, combined with the insulating properties of the bamboo grass, makes it possible to endure the harsh winters.

南部の曲家と芝棟
Nambu *Magariya* and *Shiba-mune*

南部の曲家　旧北川家住宅（みちのく民俗村・岩手県北上市、2017）
主屋から鍵形にうまやが突き出し、その入隅に入り口を設けるのが曲家の特徴
馬産が主産業であった南部地方において、人と馬がひとつ屋根の下で暮らす民家の形式

Nambu *magariya* (The former Kitagawa House, Michinoku Folklore Village, Kitakami, Iwate Pref., 2017)
The stable extends from the main house in an L shape. Having the entrance in the recess where the two join is a distinguishing feature of the *magariya*.
This type of house was designed so that people could live under the same roof as their horses, which were their main source of livelihood.

芝棟
南部地方の茅葺き屋根は芝棟が特徴である

Shiba-mune (planted ridge)
The *shiba-mune* is a distinctive feature of thatched roofs in the Nambu region.

主屋から大きく突き出たうまや 旧佐々木家 （遠野ふるさと村・岩手県遠野市、2017）
うまやと主屋の接続部に入り口がある
曲家の入隅部分の茅葺きは雨が集まって流れて、勾配も緩いので傷みやすい。杉皮を葺き込んで防水性を補強している

A stable protruding far out from the main house (The former Sasaki House, Tono Furusato Village, Tono, Iwate Pref., 2017)
The entrance is located where the main house and the stable join. Rainwater from the roof collects in the trough where the two wings of the house meet; the low pitch of the roof causes this part to decay easily, so cedar bark is mixed in the thatch to make it more water-resistant.

南部の曲家

南部地方、岩手県から青森県東部を含む地域の旧南部藩の領地には、曲家という茅葺き民家の形式が一般的である。この地方は寒冷で稲作農耕には適さないが、台地状の地形に広大な草原が広がり、古来より馬産が盛んで、南部馬という日本でも有数の農耕馬および軍馬を産してきた。その暮らしを営むための大きな茅葺き民家がつくられてきた。馬を複数飼う家も多く、主屋にも負けない立派なうまやが主屋と鍵形に接続してつくられた。これが南部の曲家である。
主屋とうまやの接続部の入隅に入り口が設けられるのが特徴。
曲家では、暮らしを支える馬をとても大切にし、大きな屋根の下、人と馬とが一体となった暮らしが営まれてきた。その接続部の土間に大きな囲炉裏を設けて、人と馬がその火で温まり、寒冷な冬を凌いできたのである。

Nambu *Magariya*

In the Nambu region, the area of Iwate and eastern Aomori prefectures that were once part of the Nambu domain, thatched houses are generally *magariya* (literally, "bent houses"). This region is too cold to be suitable for rice cultivation, but large tracts of grassland cover the plateaus, enabling the area to produce outstanding horses for agricultural and military use since ancient times. Large thatched houses were created for this purpose. Many households raised several horses and built stables so fine that they rivaled the main house, to which they were attached in an L shape, creating the Nambu *magariya*. One distinctive feature is that the entrance is located in the recessed corner where the stable and the house join. Being the people's source of livelihood, horses were carefully raised, and people and horses lived together under the same large roof. The hearth was set in the earthen-floored section where the two structures joined, so that people and horses could share the heat of the fire to get through the cold winter.

南部の芝棟集落遠景　（青森県南郷村　現八戸市、1983）

Overview of a village of thatched houses with *shiba-mune* in the Nambu region (Nango, Aomori Pref.; now part of Hachinohe, 1983)

芝棟にはさまざまな草花が生え、木も実生で生えることがある。これは周りの杉林から実生で生え、杉林と茅葺き屋根が一体となった風景をつくっている（岩手県洋野町、2011）

A wide variety of flowering plants grow on a *shiba-mune*, and even trees sometimes grow from seeds on them.
This one grew from a seed from the surrounding cedar woods, so the woods and the thatched roof form an integrated landscape. (Yono, Iwate Pref., 2011)

朽ちかけた茅葺き屋根になお咲き誇る芝棟のユリの花

The lilies of the *shiba-mune* continue to blossom even though the thatch has begun to deteriorate.

芝棟の際にマツが実生で生えることも許容するおおらかな茅葺き屋根

This generous thatched roof even allows a stray pine tree to grow at the edge of its *shiba-mune*.

裏返しに重ねた芝土の上に表を向けた芝土をのせて植え込み、その根をしっかり生やす。芝土の間にイチハツやユリや甘草や菖蒲など、根の張る草花を植え込む（青森県新郷村、2003）

Over sod laid upside down, more sod is laid face up and planted with grass that will put down strong roots. Several varieties of lily, iris, and other deep-rooted flowers are planted between the layers. (Shingo, Aomori Pref., 2003)

まず、数十cm角に野芝を土ごと根ごと切り取り、それを棟にかついで運ぶ

First, sod is cut in squares of a yard or so and carried up to the roof ridge.

切り取った芝土を裏返しにして3枚重ねとして、その重みで棟をしっかり押さえる

The cut sod is turned over and laid three layers deep to weight down the ridge.

南部の芝棟

芝棟は東日本全域にかつては広く分布していたが、近代化の中で、板や瓦や鉄板の棟に変わって次第にその姿を消しつつある。その中で、南部地方には、今でも芝棟が数多く残されている。

芝棟は、茅葺き屋根を葺き上げて、茅をへの字に曲げて棟をおさめた上に、芝土を厚くのせて棟を押さえるつくり方である。その芝土が風雨で流されないように野芝を植え込み、その根をはびこらせて棟をしっかり押さえるしくみである。あわせて、ユリ科の草花などの根の張る植物を植え、その根によって補強すると同時に、棟に花を咲かせてそれを楽しむ風流な屋根でもある。

The *Shiba-mune* of Nambu

Shiba-mune (planted ridges) were once found in many parts of eastern Japan, but with modernization, they are gradually giving way to wood, tile, and metal. In the Nambu region, however, many *shiba-mune* are still maintained.

To create a *shiba-mune*, thatch is laid up to the top of the roof, where it is bent over the ridge in an inverted V shape. Sod is laid thickly over this to hold it down. To prevent the sod from being blown or washed away, grass that grows extensive roots is planted to hold the ridge firmly in place. At the same time, various types of lilies and other flowers with strong roots are planted to reinforce the ridge and, at the same time, produce flowers that will create an elegant roof.

秋田の中門造
Akita's *Chumon-zukuri*

秋田県羽後町の中門造の集落 (2002)　　　　　　　　　A *chumon-zukuri* village in Ugo, Akita Pref. (2002)

中門造は、主屋から突き出たうまやの屋根が道路の正面に向いてつくられ、主屋の入り口も兼ねるので、屋根は正面としての意匠が凝らされる。これは、入母屋破風の中門造（秋田県羽後町、2002）

A *chumon-zukuri* house has the horse stable extending from the main house and facing the road. This also serves as the main entrance to the house, so the stable roof is elaborately designed. This is the hipped and gabled roof of a *chumon-zukuri*. (Ugo, Akita Pref., 2002)

中門造

中門造は、新潟県から秋田県までの日本海側と福島県の会津地方を含む豪雪地域に分布する。この地域は日本有数の豪雪地域であるが、同時に豊かな稲作地帯でもあり、中門造は、その豪雪と米づくりの経済力を背景に発達した民家形式である。主屋から前面の道路までの間にうまやを鍵形に曲げて延ばし、うまやの片側に通路を設けて、雪に埋もれた冬の間にも道路への出入りを確保するための工夫である。そのため、うまやの茅葺き屋根正面には玄関としての意匠が凝らされ、家格の象徴となり、地域的な特色も表している。

Chumon-zukuri

Chumon-zukuri houses are distributed in the very snowy regions from Niigata Prefecture to Akita Prefecture along the Japan Sea and into Fukushima Prefecture. While these are the snowiest parts of Japan, they are also bountiful rice-producing areas. The *chumon-zukuri* houses developed in this setting of heavy snow and economic strength from rice production. The horse stable extends in an L shape from the main house to the road in front. A corridor along the side of the stable secures passage to the road when the house is buried in snow. Because the stable wing serves as the main entrance, the front end of the roof is given an elaborate design that indicates the family's status and evidences the characteristics of the area.

甲屋根の中門造 (秋田県羽後町、2002)

Chumon-zukuri with helmet roof (*kabuto-yane*) (Ugo, Akita Pref., 2002)

屋根を数分割して、毎年順番に差し茅を施す。また、ほかに雪で傷んだ部分もあわせて差し茅をして補修する（秋田県矢島町、1980）

Each year, one section of the roof is repaired using *sashi-gaya*, and snow damage is also repaired at the same time.(Yajima, Akita Pref., 1980)

差し茅

雪の多いこの地方では、雪どけの頃、凍結によって屋根が傷むので、春には毎年差し茅をして修理するのが習わしである。

差し茅は、屋根を修理する際に古茅をおろして葺き替えるのではなく、古茅を残したまま、その間に半切りとした茅を差し込んで補強する方法である。この地方では、葺き替えることはほとんどなく、毎年行われる差し茅によって、大きな茅葺き屋根が維持されている。毎年秋に茅を刈り、その茅を主屋の外周部に立てかけて雪囲いとする。これは主屋を風雪から守り、保温する役割を果たしつつ、茅を翌年まで保管する方法である。春に雪がとけると、その茅で差し茅して屋根を補修する。雪囲いと差し茅が一体となった茅の段階的利用の知恵である。

Roof Repair (*Sashi-gaya*)

In areas where roofs are damaged by heavy snow and ice, they are repaired annually using *sashi-gaya*, a method that leaves the old thatch on the roof and inserts bunches of *kaya* (thatching material) as needed. Roofs in these areas are rarely rethatched entirely, but maintained using this method. *Kaya* harvested in the fall is stored as a snow fence to protect the main house from wind and snow and to help insulate it. After the spring thaw, this *kaya* is used to repair the roof. This resourceful system integrates two stages in the use of *kaya*.

古茅と新茅が縞状になって差し茅による修理が終わる 縞模様は風雨にさらされることによって、次第に目立たなくなる

When the repair is finished, the old and new *kaya* give the roof a striped look, but with exposure to the elements over time, the new material no longer stands out.

古茅の間に棒を差し込んで、茅を一部めくる
A rod is inserted into the roof to lift part of the old thatch.

そこに半切りとした新しい茅を差し込む
New *kaya*, cut in half, is inserted into the aperture.

先端を尖らせた細い棒を縄の先に結び付ける
A pointed stick is tied to the end of a rope.

それを針の先につけて、屋根裏に差し込む
This is then attached to the point of a needle and pushed through to the underside of the roof.

その棒が屋根裏でひっかかることによって、茅を押さえる縄を締めることができる
The stick hooks the underside of the roof, making it possible to tighten the rope that holds down the *kaya*.

茅をおしぼこで押さえ、縄で縛る
The *kaya* is then held down with a sway and tied with rope.

古茅と新しく差した茅を雁木棒で叩きそろえる
The old and new *kaya* are aligned by beating with leggets.

ハサミで平滑に刈り込む
Finally, the surface is trimmed smooth.

鈴木家住宅遠景（国指定重要文化財・秋田県羽後町、2002）
最も古い中門造のひとつ　17世紀の建築と推定されている

View of the Suzuki House (Important Cultural Property; Ugo, Akita Pref., 2002)
This is one of the oldest *chumon-zukuri*, estimated to have been built in the 17th century.

鈴木家住宅中門造正面
右端が玄関入り口
この地方を代表する旧家の家格が中門造の破風に表れている

Front view of the Suzuki House *chumon-zukuri*
The front entrance is on the right edge.
The gable of the *chumon-zukuri* attests to this old family's status as local leaders.

鈴木家住宅主屋から大きく突き出た中門造のうまや側面

The side of the *chumon-zukuri* stable projects far out from the main house (The Suzuki House).

鈴木家住宅主屋正面

Front view of the main house (The Suzuki House)

逆葺き　Reverse Thatching

大和地方のススキの逆葺き（奈良県宇陀市、2019）　Reverse thatching with miscanthus in the Nara region (Uda, Nara Pref., 2019)

大和地方のススキの逆葺き　Reverse thatching with miscanthus in the Nara region

茅葺き図鑑
Reference

山形盆地の稲ワラの逆葺き（山形県山形市、2002）

Reverse thatching with rice straw on the Yamagata plateau (Yamagata, Yamagata Pref., 2002)

茅の葺き方として、根元を下に向ける葺き方と、穂先を下に向ける葺き方の二通りがある。穂先を下に向けて葺く葺き方は、茅が逆さになるので、逆葺きと呼ばれる。茅は根元が太く丈夫で長持ちする。その根元を下、すなわち外側に向けて葺くと、茅葺きは長持ちし、厚く葺くことにも適している。今日見られる茅葺きは、厚く葺くことで居住性と耐久性に優れた真葺きが一般的となっている。一方逆葺きは、柔らかい穂先が外に出るので傷みやすいが、雨仕舞に優れ、薄葺きに向き、簡単に葺けるという利点がある。今日でも、簡易で仮設的な建物には、その利点を生かして逆葺きが用いられる。

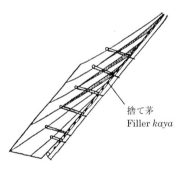

真葺き
Regular thatch

捨て茅
Filler *kaya*

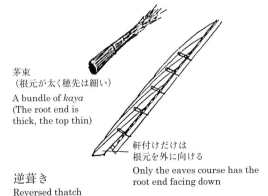

茅束
（根元が太く穂先は細い）
A bundle of *kaya*
(The root end is thick, the top thin)

軒付けだけは根元を外に向ける
Only the eaves course has the root end facing down

逆葺き
Reversed thatch

Two basic thatching methods can be found in Japan, one where the *kaya* is laid with the root end facing down and one where it is laid in reverse, with the tops facing down (*saka-buki*). Thatching with the root end down, e.g. facing outwards, creates a durable roof and is suitable for thick thatch. Most of the thatched roofs seen today are thatched thickly for livability and durability. With reverse thatching, the soft tops are on the outside making the thatch less durable, but having the advantages of being outstanding for keeping out rain, best for thin thatch, and easy to do. So even now, simple and temporary structures take advantage of these qualities and are thatched in reverse.

田麦俣のタカハッポウ造
The *Takahappo-zukuri* of Tamugimata (Yamagata Pref.)

月山の麓の急峻な山間地域に立地する田麦俣集落（山形県鶴岡市、2009）

Tamugimata is situated in a steep valley at the foot of Mt. Gassan (Tsuruoka, Yamagata Pref., 2009).

甲造の屋根裏は三層になった蚕室
サス構造を利用して、柱のない大空間をつくりあげている (2009)

A helmet roof with three stories for raising silkworms
Use of a brace structure creates a large space with no posts (2009).

屋根裏の蚕室に明かりと通風をとるために、屋根の側面両側に破風窓が設けられる (2009)

Each gable has windows to provide light and ventilation for the roof space (2009).

豪雪地帯のこの地域では、雪に埋もれても甲造の破風窓によって採光と通風の役割を果たす (1986)

The gable windows let in light and air even when the house is buried in snow (1986).

タカハッポウ造の屋根が立ち並んでいた往時の田麦俣の集落景観 (1945年頃)

View of Tamugimata as it used to look when there were many *takahappo-zukuri* (circa 1945)

田麦俣のタカハッポウ造

甲造の巨大な多層民家は、タカハッポウ造と呼ばれる。月山の麓の耕作地が狭小で急峻な山間の集落では、養蚕が暮らしを支えた。敷地が狭いので、屋根裏を最大限に活用して蚕室を拡大した結果、甲屋根の多層民家タカハッポウ造が生まれた。巨大な屋根裏に通風と採光をはかるために、妻側だけではなく、平側両面にも破風窓が付く。茅葺き屋根にこのような多くの破風窓を設けるには、高度な技術がいるが、養蚕の経済力が多くの茅葺き職人を育て、技術が磨かれ、端正で美しい甲造が生まれたのである。

The *Takahappo-zukuri* of Tamugimata

Houses with huge, multi-storied helmet roofs (*kabuto-yane*) are called *takahappo-zukuri*. With very little cultivatable land, this village in the steep valley at the foot of Mt. Gassan depended on sericulture for its livelihood. Because houses had very little land, the roof space was utilized to the maximum to raise silk worms, resulting in the creation of the multi-storied *takahappo* helmet roof. To provide ventilation and light for the huge roof space, windows were created not only in the barges but also on both sides of the roof. To make this many windows in a thatched roof demands a high level of skill. Earnings from sericulture enabled thatchers to be trained and to polish their skills to create beautiful, well-thatched roofs.

タカハッポウ造妻側正面　夏 (2009)
大きく切り上げた甲屋根が養蚕農家の特色を表している

Front view of a *takahappo-zukuri* in summer (2009)
The large, high helmet roof is typical of houses where silkworms were raised.

同左 冬 (1986)　　　　　　　　　　Same view in winter (1986)

茅場の多面的機能と炭素の循環

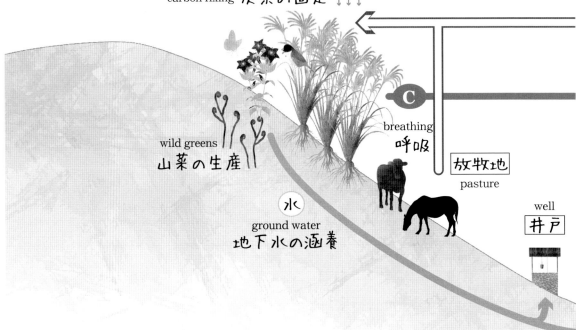

「茅場の多面的機能」

生物多様性の維持
茅場は茅のほかに、草原性の植物、昆虫、野鳥の生育をはぐくみ生物多様性の維持に大きな役割を果たす。

山菜の生産
わらびやぜんまいなどの山菜を生産する。

地下水の涵養
茅場などの草原は茂った葉で地覆し、雨水の流出と蒸発を防ぐ。また樹木に比べると蒸散する量も少ないので、地下水をよく涵養する。

炭素の固定
茅の1年間の大きな成長によって、二酸化炭素を吸収し、炭素を固定する。
年間の二酸化炭素の吸収量はスギの人工林に劣らない。

The Multifaceted Functions of *Kaya* Fields

Maintaining biodiversity
In addition to providing *kaya*, the *kaya* fields are home to grassland plants, insects, and birds, therefore play a major role in maintaining biodiversity.

Producing mountain vegetables
Kaya fields also produce edible wild greens like bracken and royal fern.

Protecting ground water
Kaya fields and other grasslands have a cover of leaves, preventing rainwater from flowing out and from evaporating. Less water evaporates than with trees, protecting underground water.

Fixing carbon
Because *kaya* grows rapidly, it absorbs carbon dioxide and fixes the carbon. The amount of carbon dioxide absorbed is comparable to that of a forest of planted cedars.

The Multifaceted Functions of *Kaya* Fields and the Carbon Cycle

茅葺き図鑑
Reference

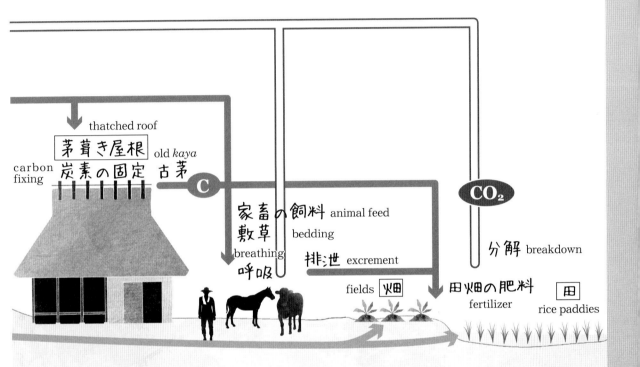

「茅の利用における炭素の循環」

野山の茅場で刈った茅は、里の民家の茅葺き屋根に葺かれ、また牛馬の敷草や飼料としても使われる。屋根の葺き替えで生じた古茅と牛馬の敷草に使われたものや、牛馬の糞はすべて回収され、田畑に肥料として施される。

それらの肥料は、バクテリアなどによって分解され、実りをもたらし、二酸化炭素が放出される。その二酸化炭素は、また春に成長する茅に吸収されて循環が巡る。

The Carbon Cycle in *Kaya* Use

Kaya harvested in the fields and hills is used in the villages to thatch houses and to bed and feed livestock. The old *kaya* from rethatched roofs, *kaya* used for animal bedding, and animal manure are all collected for use as fertilizer in the fields. Bacteria break down these fertilizers, bringing the harvest to fruition and releasing carbon dioxide. This carbon dioxide is absorbed by the *kaya* that grows in the spring, completing the cycle.

会津流の茅葺き
Aizu-Style Thatch (Fukushima Pref.)

大内宿（重要伝統的建造物群保存地区　福島県下郷町、2008）
街道沿いに寄棟屋根が建ち並ぶ東日本の農村集落の風景を今日によく残している

Ouchi Juku (Important Preservation District for Groups of Traditional Buildings, 2008)
With its hipped roofs lined up along the road, this village retains the appearance of traditional rural villages in eastern Japan.

晚秋の彩りを背景に、朝日に輝く茅葺き屋根（2012）

Thatched roofs shine in the morning sun against a backdrop of late autumn foliage (2012).

街道沿いに妻入りで建ち並ぶ茅葺きの主屋
寄棟が一般的であるが屋根裏を改造した甲屋根も見られる
（2012）

The barge entrances of thatched houses lining the road
Hipped roofs are the most common, but sometimes the roof space has been renovated to create a helmet roof (2012).

南会津の山々を背景にした雪に埋もれる水引集落 （福島県南会津町、2013）

Below the mountain of Minami Aizu, Mizuhiki village lies buried in snow (Fukushima Pref., 2013).

会津の茅葺き集落

福島県の会津地方には、東日本を代表する茅葺き集落、大内宿、前沢集落、水引集落が残されている。

大内宿は、会津の下野街道沿いの茅葺き集落であり、40棟余りの茅葺きが軒を連ねて建ち並ぶ。農家ではあるが、街道に面しているので、道沿いに座敷が配置され、街道の宿場としての役割も果たしてきた。茅葺き屋根の間に庭が設けられているところに農家の佇まいが表れている。道の両側には生活用水としての水路が流れているが、かつては道中央に大きな水路があり、家の前は農作業の前庭であった。集落中央には、本陣が設けられ、参勤交代の大名の宿泊所となっていた。

前沢集落は、街道から外れた山裾の農村集落である。明治40年の大火で家屋のほとんどが消失し、その後13軒の主屋が再建され、2軒の主屋が新築された。現在14軒の茅葺きの主屋を残す。山を背景に切妻のうまやの意匠が建ち並ぶ景観が特徴的。

水引集落は、尾瀬国立公園田代山登山口への入り口の標高800mにある山あいの集落。明治19年と29年の大火でほぼ全戸が消失し、その後に再建された7軒の茅葺き民家を今に残す。

このような会津地方では、集落近くに茅場が残り、その茅で屋根を葺き、牛馬を育て、その古茅堆肥を田畑に施すという茅の循環的利用が近年まで維持されてきた。そのことが茅葺き屋根を持続させ、今日でも茅葺きを多く残す日本有数の地域となっている。

Thatched Villages of Aizu

The Aizu region of Fukushima prefecture is home to several of the leading thatched villages in eastern Japan: Ouchi Juku, Maezawa, and Mizuhiki.

Ouchi Juku has over 40 thatched houses lined up along the Shimono Kaido road. These are farm houses, but because they face the thoroughfare, people created formal rooms and provided lodging for travelers. Befitting a farm community, gardens were grown between the thatched roofs. There are canals with water for household use on both sides of the road, but in the past, there was a large canal in the middle of the road and the front yards were spaces for farm work. In the center of the village was an official residence where warlords stayed on their way to and from their domains.

Maezawa is a farm village at a distance from the main road. In 1907, a fire destroyed most of the village, but subsequently 13 landlords rebuilt their houses and 2 new houses were constructed. Today 14 thatched houses remain, the gabled fronts of their stables creating a distinctive landscape against the backdrop of the mountains.

Mizuhiki is a mountain village located at an altitude of 800 meters at the entrance to the route for climbing Mt. Tashiro in Oze National Park. Most of the village was burned down in two major fires, in 1886 and 1896, but 7 thatched houses that were rebuilt after the fires still stand.

The Aizu region still has fields of *kaya*, which is used to thatch the roofs and raise livestock, and then reused to fertilize fields, continuing the traditional cycle of *kaya* usage. This has enabled the thatched roofs to be maintained, making this one of the country's leading areas for numbers of thatched houses.

冬の前沢集落 (重要伝統的建造物群保存地区　福島県南会津町、2012)
背後の山裾から集落を望む。雪に埋もれた茅ボッチがやっと頭を出す豪雪地帯

Maezawa in winter (Important Preservation District for Groups of Traditional Buildings, Minami Aizu, Fukushima Pref., 2012) View of the village from the mountains to the rear　A pile of stored *kaya* is barely visible in the deep snow

新緑の前沢集落 (重要伝統的建造物群保存地区　福島県南会津町、2012)　正面に中門造の切妻屋根が際立つ

Maezawa village in spring (Important Preservation District for Groups of Traditional Buildings, Minami Aizu, Fukushima Pref., 2012)　A gabled *chumon-zukuri* stands out in the foreground.

水引集落（2012）　尾瀬国立公園田代山登山口への入り口の標高800mにある山あいの集落。畑に茅が施され茅葺きと有機農業の結び付きが今日まで受け継がれている

Mizuhiki is a mountain village located at an altitude of 800 meters at the entrance to the route for climbing Mt. Tashiro in Oze National Park. *Kaya* is laid in the fields, perpetuating the close link between thatch and organic agriculture (2012).

水引集落の茅葺きはうまやが前面に突き出た中門造。通りに面したうまやの正面が玄関でもあり、茅葺きの意匠の見せ所でもある。甲屋根の形式はアズマと呼ばれる (2013)

The thatched houses of Mizuhiki are *chumon-zukuri* having the stable wing jutting out to the front facing the road. This is the main entrance, so the roof is designed to show it off (2013).

大桃の舞台 (国指定重要有形民俗文化財・福島県南会津町、2010)
大桃の駒嶽神社の境内にある農村舞台で、森の木立の中に静かに建つ。甲造の茅葺き屋根

Omomo Stage (Important Tangible Folk-Cultural Property; Minami Aizu, Fukushima Pref., 2010)
This rural stage with its thatched helmet roof stands quietly in the wooded precincts of Komadake Shrine.

水引集落の中門造の茅葺き民家。切妻形式のものはキリヤと呼ばれる（2013）
A *chumon-zukuri* thatched house in Mizuhiki (2003)

水引集落
葺き替えに備えて前年の秋に刈り取った茅。茅ボッチにして冬を越す（2010）
Mizuhiki village
The *kaya* harvested the previous autumn is stored in stacks through the winter in preparation for rethatching (2010).

会津流茅葺きの特徴

会津盆地は雪が多い地域である一方、それによる水資源が豊かで夏も高温になるので、日本有数の稲作地帯である。それに加えて畜産や養蚕も盛んであったので、豊かな農業経営が営まれ、それを背景として、大きく立派な茅葺き民家がつくられた。

日本海側に近い会津の西部地域の前沢集落、水引集落は豪雪地帯で、中門造であるのに対して、雪がさほどではない会津東部地域の大内宿は直屋造である。中門造が雪国に適応したつくりであることが、これによっても理解できる。

棟仕舞は、もともとくれぐしと呼ばれる芝棟が一般的であったが、次第に杉皮を被せて千木をのせた形式への変遷が見られる。

Characteristics of Aizu-Style Thatch

The Aizu basin gets a lot of snow, which makes it rich in water resources. At the same time, it also gets hot in summer, making it one of Japan's leading rice-producing areas. In addition, animal husbandry and sericulture flourished. The wealth thus obtained enabled people to build fine, large thatched houses.

In the western part of Aizu, near the Japan Sea, Maezawa and Mizuhiki get lots of snow and therefore created *chumon-zukuri*. In contrast, Ouchi Juku in the eastern part of Aizu does not get much snow, so the houses were built straight. This should make it clear why the *chumon-zukuri* were adapted to snowy regions. Originally, planted ridges were common, but this gradually changed to a ridge covered with cedar bark held down with *chigi*.

檜枝岐の舞台（国指定重要有形民俗文化財　福島県檜枝岐村、2010）
檜枝岐は沼田街道の南の玄関口。江戸時代から鎮守神祭礼の奉納芝居として認められ伝承されてきた檜枝岐歌舞伎が、春の愛宕祭と秋の鎮守祭に奉納される。甲造の茅葺き屋根で棟はくれぐし

Stage at Hinoemata (Important Tangible Folk-Cultural Property; Hinoemata, Fukushima Pref., 2010)
Hinoemata is the south entrance to the Numata Highway. Since the Edo period (1603-1868), Hinoemata Kabuki has been handed down as a performance dedicated to the protecting gods and it is still performed at religious ceremonies in spring and fall. The stage has a thatched helmet roof with a planted ridge.

前沢集落のくれぐしの水車小屋（2010）

A waterwheel house with a planted ridge in Maezawa village (2010)

旧五十嵐家住宅（国指定重要文化財　福島県只見町、2011）
享保3年に建築された県内では最も古い民家。奥会津の古い曲家の形式を伝える。棟は置千木

The former Igarashi House (Important Cultural Property; Tadami, Fukushima Pref., 2011)
Built in 1718, it is the oldest house in the prefecture and shows the style of the Aizu *magariya* at the time. The ridge is finished with *chigi*.

前沢集落の倉。倉の屋根は茅葺きの置屋根で、急勾配の茅葺き屋根が緩い土蔵の屋根にのるので、そこに三角形の隙間が生じる。茅葺きの屋根が軽やかに見える（2013）

Storehouse in Maezawa　The steep-pitched thatched over-roof rests on the low-pitched roof of the storehouse, creating a triangular space that gives the thatched roof a light-weight appearance (2013).

大内宿の茅場（ふるさと文化財の森　福島県下郷町、2014）

Kaya field at Ouchi Juku (Furusato Bunkazai no Mori., Shimogo, Fukushima Pref., 2014)

大内宿の屋根葺き（2010）
集落のユイと、地元の職人グループの共同で屋根が毎年2〜3軒ずつ葺き替えられる

Thatching at Ouchi Juku (2010)
Every year, two or three roofs are thatched through the joint effort of the village system of cooperative labor and a local group of thatchers.

刈った茅はニュウにしてその場で春先まで乾燥させる（2012）

The harvested *kaya* is arranged in stacks and left to dry until spring (2012).

秋に刈った茅は、よいものとよくないものに選別し、よくない茅は、牛馬の敷草にし、よいものは、雪囲いや茅ニュウとして保管する。雪囲いは、主屋や土蔵に立てかけて、冬期間茅を保管するとともに、建物を雪から守り、断熱材として保温する役割を果たす。
春には、それらの茅を使って屋根を葺く。屋根からおろした古茅は、傷みの少ないものは屋根に再利用し、傷んだものは田畑に施す。

The *kaya* harvested in the fall is separated by quality. Substandard *kaya* is used to bed livestock, while good *kaya* is stacked or made into snow fences. Snow fences are stood around houses and storehouses, thereby storing the *kaya* over the winter and at the same time protecting the structures from snow and helping insulate them.
In spring, this *kaya* is used to thatch the roofs. When the old *kaya* is stripped from the roof, that in good condition is reused on the new roof, while damaged *kaya* is put in the fields.

北上川のヨシ原　Yoshi (Reed) Beds in the Kitakami River (Miyagi Pref.)

北上川河口に広がるヨシ原（宮城県石巻市、2002）　　Yoshi at the mouth of the Kitakami River (Ishinomaki, Miyagi Pref., 2002)

かつての刈り取り風景。現在は大型機械を導入して刈り取りが行われている（2002）　　Harvesting yoshi in the past. Now a large machine is used (2002).

茅葺き図鑑
Reference

汐の干潮を利用して刈り取りが行われ、かつては、満ち潮のときに船で岸まで運んだ（2002）

Harvesting takes advantage of low tide; in the past, the reed was carried to shore by boat at high tide (2002).

北上川河口には日本でも有数の汽水域のヨシ原が広がっている。管理されているヨシ原の面積は約140haで、そのうち70〜80haで刈り取りが行われている。北上川周辺の10集落によって管理され、契約講による集落の利用者や地元の業者によってヨシが刈り取られ、利用されている。刈り取り時期は12月中旬から3月で、4月中旬に野焼きされヨシ原が維持されている。2011年の震災による津波の被害を受け、現在は2尺〆で約1万束の収穫量で、震災前の2分の1〜3分の1に減少したが、利用者や支援者の協力によって、ヨシ原の再生の取り組みがすすめられている。このヨシの生い茂る汽水域は、ベッコウシジミやサケ、サクラマスなどの水産資源にも恵まれ、地域の暮らしを支えている。また、風にそよぐヨシ原の葉音は「残したい音風景100選」にも選定されている。

The area at the mouth of the Kitakami River has one of Japan's largest brackish-water *yoshi* (reed) beds. About 140ha are managed *yoshi* beds, of which 70~80ha are harvested. Ten villages near the river supervise the beds, which are used under contract with villagers and local businesses. The reed beds are maintained by harvesting from mid-December through March, then burning off in mid-April. Badly damaged by the tsunami following the Great East Japan Earthquake in 2011, present harvests amount to about 10,000 bundles 2 feet in circumference, about a half or a third of what they were before the disaster, but through the cooperative effort of local users and their supporters, progress is being made in restoring the reed beds. The brackish water where reeds thrive is rich in freshwater clams and other aquatic resources that support life in the area. The sound of *yoshi* blowing in the wind has been designated one of the "100 Soundscapes for Preservation," and hopefully the *yoshi* beds will rejuvenate.

ヨシ原の多面的機能と炭素の循環

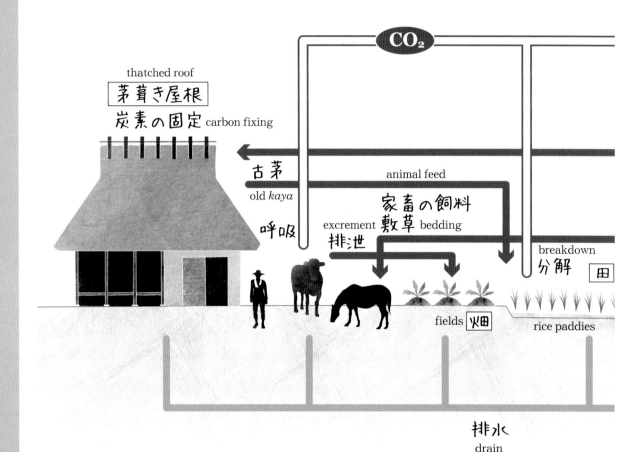

「ヨシ原の多面的機能」

生物多様性の維持
ヨシ原はヨシのほかに湿原性の植物、昆虫や野鳥、水生生物の生育をはぐくみ生物多様性の維持に大きな役割を果たす。

水産資源の涵養
魚介類の産卵場、棲家となり、豊かな水産資源をはぐくむ。

水質浄化
ヨシは成長する過程で窒素やリンなどの汚れを栄養分として吸収する。ヨシ原の水中の茎や根元についた微生物が汚れを分解する。そのヨシを刈り取って使うことで、水質浄化は促進される。

炭素の固定
ヨシの1年間の大きな成長によって、二酸化炭素を吸収し、炭素を固定する。

The Multifaceted Functions of Reed Beds

Maintaining biodiversity
In addition to providing *yoshi*, the reed beds are home to aquatic plants, insects, and birds, thereby playing a major role in maintaining biodiversity.

Producing of aquatic resources

In the process of growing, reed absorbs pollutants like nitrogen and phosphorus as nutrients. Microorganisms on the roots and underwater stems break down the pollutants. Thus, maintaining the reed beds by harvesting and using the reed, promotes water purification.

Fixing carbon
Because *yoshi* grows rapidly, it absorbs carbon dioxide and fixes the carbon.

The Multifaceted Functions of Reed Beds and the Carbon Cycle

茅葺き図鑑 Reference

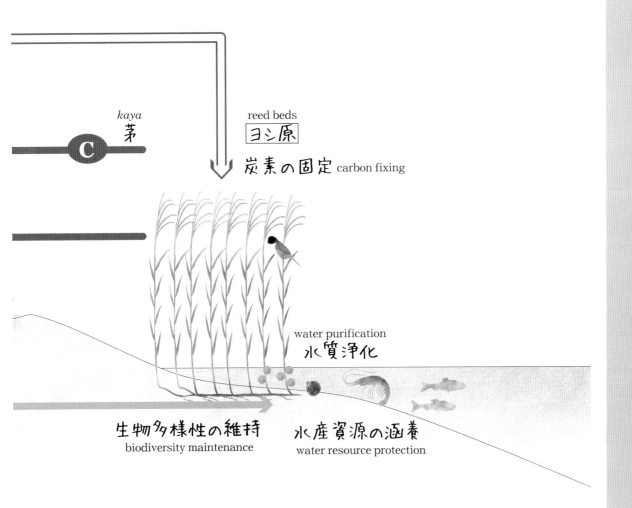

「ヨシの利用における炭素の循環」

水辺で刈ったヨシは、里の民家の茅葺き屋根に葺かれ、また牛馬の敷草や飼料としても使われる。屋根の葺き替えで生じた古茅と牛馬の敷草に使われたものや、牛馬の糞はすべて回収され、田畑に肥料として施される。

それらの肥料は、バクテリアなどによって分解され、実りをもたらし、二酸化炭素が放出される。その二酸化炭素は、また春に成長するヨシに吸収されて循環が巡る。

The Carbon Cycle in Reed Use

The reed harvested at the water's edge is used in the villages to thatch houses and to bed and feed livestock. As with other types of *kaya*, old reed from rethatched roofs, reed used for animal bedding, and animal manure are all collected for use as fertilizer in the fields. Bacteria break down these fertilizers, bringing the harvest to fruition and releasing carbon dioxide. This carbon dioxide is absorbed by the reed that grows in the spring, completing the cycle.

筑波山麓　石岡市八郷地区の茅葺き民家（茨城県石岡市、2009）
背後にスギやケヤキの屋敷林、主屋と書院のふたつの茅葺き屋根がのぞく

筑波流の茅葺き
Tsukuba-Style Thatch (Ibaraki Pref.)

Thatched houses in the Yasato section of Ishioka at the foot of Mt. Tsukuba (2009)
The thatched roofs of the main and guest houses can be seen beyond the stand of cedar and zelkova trees protecting the property.

正面が主屋、左が書院 (2006)

The main house is in front, with the guest house to the left (2006).

屋根の隅で軒の高さが異なる部分に特別なおさめ方が必要
三面といわれる装飾的な技巧が施される

Where the height of the eaves differs, a special decorative technique is needed to finish the corners.

山裾に広がる水田の向こうにイグネと屋敷林に囲われた茅葺き民家
(2006)

Across the rice paddies, at the foot of the mountain, can be seen a thatched house surrounded by a hedge and a stand of trees (2006).

左が書院で右が主屋 (2006)
書院の前には日本庭園がつくられる

The guest house is on the left and the main house on the right (2006). A formal Japanese garden has been created in front of the guest house.

国指定史跡佐久良東雄旧宅(茨城県石岡市、2006)
茅葺きの長屋門と背後に見える主屋

The former home of Azumao Sakura (National Historic Site, Ishioka, Ibaraki Pref., 2006)
The gatehouse and the main house beyond it are both thatched.

長屋門から主屋を望む(2006)

The main house seen from the gatehouse (2006)

石岡市八郷地区の大場ぶどう園主屋（国登録有形文化財、2019）

The main house at the Oba Vineyard (Registered Tangible Cultural Property, Yasato, Ishioka, 2019)

主屋の軒下の縁側と土間入り口には正月の門松が飾られている（2019）

The porch under the eaves of the main house and New Year decorations at the entrance to the earthen-floored section (2019)

築約150年の主屋の小屋組 (2013)
筑波山麓の豊富なマツの材を活用して、二重、三重にマツ梁を組んで広い土間空間を支える

The truss of the main house, built about 150 years ago (2013)
Utilizing the plentiful pine timber at the foot of Mt. Tsukuba, the truss was built in two and three layers to support the large earthen-floored space.

筑波流の茅葺き

筑波山麓の農村集落は、里山の資源と温暖な気候に恵まれ、稲作と合わせて小麦の二毛作、それに加えて果樹や園芸作物など多様な農業経営が営まれてきた。その経済力を背景に、会津地方からも茅葺きの出稼ぎ職人が多数出入りし、地元の職人と競合して切磋琢磨された結果、筑波流茅手が生まれた。

主屋のほかに、書院と呼ばれる離れがあり、離れは客間であると同時に、老夫婦の居室としても使われる。そのほかに、納屋や倉や長屋門も茅葺きであったので、屋敷内には数棟の茅葺きが群を成した農村景観をつくりあげている。また、筑波山からの季節風をよけるために、北西側には屋敷林、隣地との境界や南面はイグネと呼ばれるカシやモチの垣根で囲われ、それらと茅葺き屋根が調和した美しい風景が特色となっている。

戦中戦後の食料増産の時代には、二毛作として小麦栽培が奨励され、農地が拡大され茅場が減少した結果、多くの茅葺き屋根は小麦ワラで葺かれた。小麦ワラは茅に比べると耐久性が短く、頻繁な葺き替えが必要となるが、それを支える職人集団が腕を競い合い、日本でも有数の技巧的な技が発達したのが筑波流の茅葺き屋根である。また、小麦ワラ葺きの頻繁な葺き替えは、大量の古茅肥料をもたらし、それが農業生産を高める好循環を生み、「屋根を葺けば米がとれる」といわれてきた。

Tsukuba-Style Thatch

Blessed with nearby woodland resources and a mild climate, the rural villages at the foot of Mt. Tsukuba have been able to undertake a variegated agriculture, growing rice coupled with double crops of wheat, as well as fruit and horticultural produce. The wealth thus obtained enabled many thatchers to journey from the Aizu area to work in competition with local thatchers, thus creating the Tsukuba-style thatcher.

In addition to the main house, a separate structure served as a room for guests and also as living space for elderly parents. In addition to these, barns, storehouses, and gatehouses are also thatched, creating a rural landscape made up of properties with groups of numerous thatched buildings. Other local features are the stands of trees to the northwest side of the properties to ward off the winter winds from Mt. Tsukuba and hedges of live oak and other plants between properties and to the south, which blend with the thatched roofs to form a distinctive landscape.

During and after World War II, when food production was being increased, double crops of wheat were promoted and farmland was expanded, reducing the *kaya* fields. In consequence, many roofs were thatched with wheat straw. Wheat straw is not as durable as other *kaya* and requires frequent rethatching, but the groups of thatchers who supported the roofs competed, raising the level of skill to make Tsukuba-style roofs among the finest workmanship in the country. Frequent rethatching also generated large quantities of thatch fertilizer, creating a virtuous cycle that increased agricultural production so much that people said "If you thatch the roof, you get a rice harvest."

保存会と市民ボランティアが毎年3日間、延べ100〜200名参加して茅刈りが行われている

The Yasato *Kayabuki Yane Hozon Kai* and citizen volunteers, about 100 to 200 people altogether, spend 3 days every year harvesting *kaya*.

筑波山麓の茅刈り

筑波山麓でも近年茅葺き民家が減少した結果、里山の茅場はほとんど失われている。その存続を救ったのが、筑波研究学園都市の研究所に自生した茅場である。研究所では、地下に設けた実験施設の保全のために、毎年地上の雑草や雑木を駆除した結果、良好なススキの茅場が生まれた。そこで、やさと茅葺屋根保存会では、残された茅葺き屋根を守るために、茅場としての利用を研究所に求め、研究所も地域の文化を守るためと茅の有効利用をはかるため、茅場としての利用が実現し、茅葺き所有者や地域住民による共同の茅刈りが毎年継続されている。

Tsukuba *Kaya* Harvest

Because of the decline in the number of thatched houses in recent years, most of the *kaya* fields on the local hills at the foot of Mt. Tsukuba have disappeared. But the *kaya* growing at the research laboratories of Tsukuba Science City has come to the rescue. To protect the underground research facilities, the grasses and trees above them are cut down annually, creating a field of good *susuki* for thatching. The Yasato *Kayabuki Yane Hozon Kai* (The society to preserve Yasato's thatched roofs) got permission from the research institute to use this *kaya* to preserve the remaining thatched houses, and every year the local citizens and owners of thatched houses have been cooperating to harvest the *kaya*.

コマルキ
屋根を葺くために茅を束ね直す　穂先をあわせて束ねてふたつに切った胴切りと呼ばれる切り茅をこしらえる様子
屋根には長い茅と切り茅を交互に重ねて葺く

Kaya is rebundled for thatching. Here the tops are aligned in a bundle that is then cut in two, creating cut *kaya*.
Long and cut *kaya* are laid on alternately when thatching.

最高のキリトビの文様　松竹梅　　　　　　　　The best *kiritobi* design: pine-bamboo-plum

茅束のマクラでキリトビの小口を大きくせり出して誇張したタコドメ
文字は小さく寿

A *kaya* pillow is used to make the *kiritobi* stand out. The character for longevity has been cut small.

茅葺きを火から守る祈りが込められ龍の文字が刻まれる

The character for dragon has been carved to pray for protection against fire.

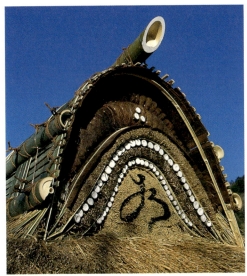

火伏せの祈りが込められた水の装飾文字

The character for water is carved into the *kiritobi* as a prayer to ward off fire.

竹簀巻きとキリトビ

この地域の棟は、棟茅を高く積み上げて竹簀で巻いてつくられる。その棟の小口を切ってとめるという意味で、キリトメ転じてキリトビの棟と呼ばれる。稲ワラを高く積み上げて棟の端を反り上げて大きな小口をつくり、それを杉皮と竹で巻いて補強する。その棟の小口に屋根バサミで文様を切り込み、墨入れ彩色を施して装飾的に小口を飾るのである。装飾の文様としては、「寿」などの吉祥文字や、火除けとしての「龍」、「水」などの文字が刻まれるほかに、松竹梅、菊水などの縁起の良い文様も描かれる。この地域の屋根は素朴な寄棟の形式であるが、棟を高く反り上げ、その小口が屋根全体を引き締め、遠くからもその文様が楽しめるのである。

Takesu-maki and *Kiritobi*

In this area, the ridges of the houses are created by piling the ridge *kaya* high and covering it with an arrangement of bamboo slats called *takesu*. The ends of the ridge are cut off, from which comes the name *kiritome* or *kiritobi* ridge. To make these, rice straw is piled high, curving the edge of the ridge upwards to create a large end. This is reinforced with a cover of cedar bark and bamboo. With shears, designs are cut into the ridge end and colored with black ink for decoration. The designs may be Chinese characters for good fortune, such as "longevity," or characters like "dragon" or "water" to ward off fire, or they may depict the propitious pine-bamboo-plum or floating chrysanthemum motifs. The roofs in this area are simple hipped roofs, but the ridges bent upwards with the end designs bring the whole together and can be enjoyed from a distance.

軒付けトオシモノの1段ごとに尺八と呼ばれる細い竹で補強して、軒を大きく張り出す

The first eaves course is reinforced with an arrangement of thin pieces of bamboo, which enables the eaves to extend far out.

7層のトオシモノ (2010)
最下層の白いのは稲ワラ、黒いのは古茅、灰色のは新茅の縞模様 最後に杉皮を並べて防水。その上の水切り茅のみを葺き替える

Seven-layer eaves (2010)
The lowest, white layer is rice straw; the dark layers, old *kaya*; and the medium-light ones, new *kaya*. Atop the striped under-eaves is laid a course of cedar bark for waterproofing. Only the layers above the bark are rethatched.

竹簀の子で棟を巻いて、根元を縄で強く締め上げる (2006)

The ridge is covered with a mat of bamboo slats and tied down very securely with rope (2006).

刈り込みながら屋根足場をはずしていく (2006)

The footing poles are removed as the thatchers trim the roof from the top down (2006).

軒付け　トオシモノ

筑波流茅手の技の特徴のひとつに、幾層にも葺き重ねられた軒付けトオシモノがある。トオシモノは、最下層に稲ワラを敷き並べ、その上に古い茅、新しい茅、そしてまた古い茅、新しい茅として縞模様をつくり、軒裏を美しく飾ると同時に、古茅を再利用する技でもある。その層は、3層、5層から9層まで奇数でつくられ、層が多いほど手間がかかる高級な屋根とされる。この軒付けの上に杉皮で防水をし、その上に水切り茅を葺き重ねて軒付けが完成する。杉皮から下の部分は、基本的には葺き替えることはなく、水切り茅から上だけが葺き替えられる。この軒付けに屋根全体の半分の手間がかかるといわれるほど丁寧につくり、また長くもたせるのである。

Multilayered Eaves

One of the characteristic techniques of the Tsukuba-style thatcher is the multi-layered eaves, which create a striped effect, with rice straw for the bottom layer followed by a course of old *kaya*, then one of new *kaya*, then another of old *kaya*, and again new *kaya*. This creates beautiful eaves and also is a way to reuse old kaya. The layers are made in odd numbers: 3, 5, or even 9. The more layers, the more work they involve, hence the higher the grade of the roof. Over these, a course of cedar bark is laid as waterproofing, then the outermost eaves course is laid to complete the eaves. In general, the courses below the cedar bark are permanent and only the thatch above the bark is replaced. The carefully made eaves are said to involve half of the total work on the roof and are made to last a long time.

霞ヶ浦のヨシ原 The *Yoshi* (Reed) Bed of Lake Kasumigaura

霞ヶ浦湖畔のヤーラ　　　　　　　　　　　　　*Yara* on the shore of Lake Kasumigaura

バインダーで刈り取った束数把をワラで1束にまとめる　　Several of the bundles cut by machine are bound into one bundle with rice-straw rope.

茅葺き図鑑
Reference

霞ヶ浦湖畔の野焼き（茨城県稲敷市、2003）
ほかの植物の侵入を防いで良質な茅を維持するために毎年3月に行われてきた
Burning off the *kaya* beds on the shore of Lake Kasumigaura (Inashiki, Ibaraki Pref., 2003) This is done annually in March to maintain the quality of the *kaya* and prevent other plants from invading.

シマガヤの茅束
A bundle of *shimagaya*

シマガヤ

シマガヤとは、霞ヶ浦の湖畔全域に自生する草であるクサヨシやカモノハシやチゴザサの茅の総称である。丈は0.7〜1.6m程度と短いが、茎は細く中空で上質な茅として利用されてきた。このようなシマガヤとヨシ原が混じる草原はヤーラと呼ばれ、この湖岸の原風景であった。現在は干拓や護岸工事によって、ヤーラの多くは失われたが、一部数haで今日も茅刈りが行われ、地域の茅葺き屋根に葺かれている。平坦な茅場であり、また細く短い茅なので、稲刈り用のバインダーで効率よく刈り取ることができる。毎年春に火入れが行われ、良質な茅が再生産されてきた。このヤーラが失われその茅刈りも減少したことによって、霞ヶ浦の水質が悪化し、ヨシ原に生息する希少な動植物も失われ、その保全と再生のためにもヤーラと茅葺き屋根の復活が求められている。

Shimagaya

Shimagaya is the generic term for the reed and duckbill grasses that grow around the shores of Lake Kasumigaura. Measuring about 1 to 1.5 meters, *shimagaya* is relatively short, but the hollow stems make it a good-quality *kaya*. The areas where *shimagaya* and reed beds mix, called *yara*, create the original landscape of the lakeside. Many *yara* have been lost due to draining and embankments, but *shimagaya* is still harvested on a few hectares for thatching local roofs. Because the thatch field is flat and the *kaya* is fine, it can be harvested efficiently with the reaper used for harvesting rice. The *kaya* beds are burned off every spring, so good-quality *kaya* is reproduced. Due to the loss of the *yara* and the decline in harvesting *kaya*, the quality of the water in Kasumigaura has deteriorated, and rare plants and animals have been lost. To save these and improve the quality of the lake, it is hoped that the *yara* and thatched roofs will be rejuvenated.

関東山地の甲屋根
The Helmet Roofs of the Kanto Mountains

内田家住宅（国指定重要文化財・埼玉県秩父市、2018）

The Uchida House (Important Cultural Property; Chichibu, Saitama Pref., 2018)

関東山地の甲屋根

関東地方の北西部の埼玉県、栃木県、群馬県、東京都にかけての山岳地帯は関東山地と呼ばれ、上越の国境の山々に連なる奥深いところである。

この山岳地帯では、豊富な森林資源のほかに、古来より養蚕業の一大中心地として繁栄してきた。茅葺き民家の屋根裏で養蚕業を行うために、屋根裏を拡大して採光と通風をはかる甲屋根が、各地で多様に発達している。

甲屋根とは、元々寄棟屋根の妻側を台形状に切り上げて、その形がかぶとに見えることから、甲屋根と呼ばれる。妻側が甲屋根になるのが一般的であるが、群馬県では平側前面を大きく甲屋根とした雄大な屋根が特徴的である。

また、埼玉県の奥地である秩父地方や東京都の奥多摩地方では、元々入母屋屋根であった茅葺き屋根に、甲屋根としての改造を重ねた結果、二重甲という複雑で独自な屋根が発達した。養蚕業の繁栄を背景として、その地域の茅葺き屋根のかたちをそれぞれ独自な工夫を凝らした結果が、この多様な甲屋根の民家群をつくりあげたのである。また、養蚕の経済力は、雪国の越後地方などからの出稼ぎの茅葺き職人を受入れ、職人の層も厚く、甲屋根の改造の切磋琢磨が生まれ、装飾豊かな破風窓が養蚕農家の繁栄の証として雄大な甲屋根に彩りを添えている。

The Helmet Roofs of the Kanto Mountains

The northwestern part of the Kanto plain, extending from the Joetsu (Niigata) border through Gunma, Tochigi, and Saitama prefectures and into western Tokyo is a deeply mountainous area. In addition to having bountiful timber resources, it has flourished from ancient times as a major center of the silk industry. In order to raise silk worms in the roof space, helmet roofs were created throughout the region to enlarge the space under the roofs and let in light and air.

They were made by cutting trapezoid-shaped windows in the barge end of what were originally hipped roofs, making them look like a warrior's helmet, hence the name. Generally the helmet roof was made on the barge, but in Gunma, a huge helmet created on the long side of the roof is characteristic.

In Chichibu, deep in the mountains of Saitama prefecture, and in the Okutama area of Tokyo, hipped and gabled roofs were repeatedly renovated, eventually resulting in complicated, unique two-layer helmet roofs. The prosperity from the silk industry enabled each area to work out distinctive roof shapes, resulting in a variety of helmet-roof houses. The sericulture economy enabled the area to accept thatchers journeying from the snowy Echigo (Niigata) region, creating an abundance of thatchers, who rivaled each other to renovate the helmet roofs, thus leading to the decorative windows in the enormous roofs that bore testimony to the prosperity of the sericulture farmers.

大きく切り上がった平甲の屋根　　Helmet roof cut high into the long side of the roof

兜家旅館の二重甲屋根（東京都檜原村、2009） The two-tiered helmet roof of the Kabutoya Inn (Hinohara, Tokyo, 2009)

たから温泉の二重甲屋根　茅に上に杉皮を葺き重ねる（東京都檜原村、2009）

The two-tiered helmet roof of the Takara Hotspring *Kaya* is covered with cedar bark.(Hinohara, Tokyo, 2009)

奥多摩地方の茅と杉皮の重ね葺きの置千木の民家 (2009)　　House in Okutama thatched with *kaya* covered with cedar bark and having *chigi* logs on the ridge (2009)

茅と杉皮の重ね葺きの破風 (2009)　　A barge having *kaya* covered with cedar bark (2009)

クリの千木　表面の杉皮が苔むして風情がある（2009）
関東山地は豊かな木材資源を生かした太い千木で棟を押さえる
千木の材料には、耐久性のあるクリが用いられる

Chestnut *chigi* (2009)
Utilizing the plentiful lumber resources of the area, roofs are held down with thick *chigi* of durable chestnut. A covering of moss adds charm to this roof thatched with cedar bark.

関東山地における茅葺き材料の変遷

養蚕を営むには、蚕の飼料となる桑の枝葉の大量の採取が必要となる。

そのための桑畑が周辺の山裾に拡大していく。その結果、茅場は縮小を余儀なくされ、屋根が拡大することも重なって、茅の不足が生じた。そこで、寒冷なこの地域で明治時代以降に食料として生産が増大してきた小麦の殻を屋根に使うようになった。小麦ワラは、それまでの茅の材料であるススキに比べると半分以下の耐久性しかないが、食料生産の副産物であり、養蚕の経済力で職人を雇うことは困難ではなかったので、小麦ワラの茅葺き屋根が普及することとなった。小麦ワラは茅に比べると細く短くしなやかで、細かな茅葺き屋根の細工に向いているので、破風窓や甲屋根周りの複雑なかたちをつくりあげるのに適していた。頻繁な葺き替えのたびにその技が凝らされ、美しく技巧的な茅葺きが競うようにつくられていったのである。

一方奥多摩地方では、薪炭林にかわって、下流域の首都圏の戦後の復興資材としてスギが大量に植林され、その杉皮が大量に得られることから、小麦ワラとともに、茅葺きを杉皮葺きで覆ったものや、茅と杉皮を交互に葺き重ねた混ぜ葺きが奥多摩地方に出現した。その茅葺きに杉皮を混ぜ合わせた屋根は、50年以上の耐久性を持つことから、大きな養蚕農家の屋根として採用された。小麦ワラの生産が低下し、スギの植林が拡大された近年において、この地域の茅葺き屋根の最後のかたちとして今も受け継がれている。

Changes in Thatching Materials in the Kanto Mountains

Raising silkworms required gathering a great quantity of mulberry branches with leaves. Because of this, mulberry orchards expanded around the foot of the hills. The resulting shrinking of *kaya* fields, combined with the expanded size of the roofs, created a *kaya* shortage. Starting in the Meiji period (1868-1912), this cold area increased wheat production for food and began to use the wheat straw to thatch the roofs. Wheat straw thatch lasts only about half as long as the *susuki* that was previously used, but as a byproduct of food production, and because sericulture meant that there was no economic problem with hiring thatchers, the use of wheat straw for thatch spread. Because wheat straw is thinner, shorter, and more pliant than *susuki*, it was suited for the delicate work involved in creating the complicated shapes around gable windows and helmet roofs. Every time the roof was rethatched, the workmanship got more elaborate, and thatched roofs vied with each other for beauty and intricacy.

In the meanwhile, the Okutama region switched from forests for charcoal and kindling to lumber for the postwar rebuilding of the Tokyo area downstream. Huge areas were devoted to growing cedar for reconstruction, making a great quantity of cedar bark available. Wheat-straw roofs came to be covered with cedar bark, or *kaya* and bark were laid on the roof in alternate courses, resulting in mixed thatch appearing in this area. Because this mixed thatch with cedar bark lasts for over 50 years, it was adopted for the large roofs of houses producing silk, and seems to be the final form of the area's thatched roofs now that wheat production has dwindled and cedar groves have expanded.

苔むした杉皮の表面にユリが咲く（東京都青梅市、2018）

Lilies bloom on the moss-covered surface of this thatched roof. (Ome, Tokyo, 2018)

宮崎家住宅（国指定重要文化財・東京都青梅市、2009）
茅と杉皮を交互に葺き重ねる

The Miyazaki House (Important Cultural Property; Ome, Tokyo, 2009) This roof is thatched with alternating courses of *kaya* and cedar bark.

宮崎家の破風と棟

The gable and ridge of the Miyazaki House

秩父の三峰神社を司る社家の住宅（埼玉県秩父市、2018）
格式の高い入母屋屋根となっている

The home of the priestly family that administers Mitsumine Shrine (Chichibu, Saitama Pref., 2018)
It has a high-status hipped and gabled roof.

関東山地の中央に位置する三峰神社。その神領社家の千木は格別に大きい。屋根の中部まで及ぶ巨大な千木がどっしりとのっている

Mitsumine Shrine is situated in the center of the Kanto mountains. The house of the chief priest has especially large *chigi*, which rest solidly on the ridge and extend down to the middle of the roof.

千木は守りのしるし

千木は東北地方から九州地方にかけての山間地域に広く分布している茅葺き民家の普遍的な棟仕舞である。

千木には古来より魔除けの祈りがあるとされ、三峰神社ではオオカミが守護神である。山の暮らしにとって、オオカミはイノシシやシカなどの害獣から暮らしを守る守り神であった。そのオオカミの守護の象徴が千木なのである。

Chigi Symbolize Protection

From ancient times, *chigi* have been considered to embody a prayer for protection from evil spirits and to symbolize the wolf, which is the guardian deity of Mitsumine Shrine. For people living in the mountains, the wolf was a god who protected them from dangerous animals. Thus, *chigi* are a symbol of protection.
Chigi are a common way of finishing off the roofs of folk houses and are widely distributed in mountainous areas from Tohoku to Kyushu.

秩父地方の小麦ワラの葺き替え（埼玉県小鹿野町、2009）

Rethatching with wheat straw in the Chichibu area (Ogano, Saitama, 2009)

小麦ワラの葺き替え
Rethatching with wheat straw

小麦ワラの束
長さは90cm程度の古い品種の小麦ワラを用いる。収穫して脱穀した束をそのまま使える。麦ワラはストローに用いられるように中空で水切れがよい

A bundle of wheat straw
An old variety of wheat that has stems about 90 cm. long is used. The harvested bundle can be used as is after threshing. Wheat stems are hollow and water runs off easily.

小麦ワラで葺かれた諏訪神社全景
(秩父市小鹿野町、2018)
View of Suwa Shrine thatched with wheat straw (Ogano, Chichibu, 2018)

細かな細工に適した小麦ワラの技巧的な破風と棟の妻飾り
入母屋の破風が蓑甲にかたどられ、妻飾りに扇の文様が彫り込まれている（2009）

Elaborate decoration on the barge and ridge using wheat straw, which is well suited to this kind of craftsmanship (2009)
The hipped and gabled roof takes the shape of a covering helmet with a fan design carved into the barge decoration.

富士山麓の茅場　The *Kaya* Fields at the Foot of Mt. Fuji (Shizuoka Pref.)

土場に集められ出荷を待つ茅束。刈り取った茅はその日の内に土場へ運搬され、約200束を島にして立てておく

Bundles of *kaya* assembled for shipment　On the day it is harvested, the *kaya* is taken to the shipping yard, where it is assembled in stands of about 200 bundles.

富士山の裾野に広がる大野原は、古くは富士の巻狩りなどが行われた狩場で、明治時代は陸軍の、現在は自衛隊の演習場として利用されながら、東富士入会組合によって古くから続く入会の茅刈りが行われてきた。8900haの演習場の内、6000haが茅場で、うち3600haの範囲で200haを茅場として利用。刈り取り時期は12月〜2月で50日程度行う。9割が鎌による手刈り。収穫量は、2尺〆の手刈りの中束が3万束、3尺〆の機械刈りの大束が2万束、計約5万束。2月下旬に野焼きが行われる。東日本最大のススキの茅場。

In olden times, the vast grasslands at the foot of Mt. Fuji were hunting grounds, but in the Meiji Period (1868-1912) the area was used for military maneuvers by the army, and it is now used for practice by the Self Defense Forces. At the same time, communal *kaya* harvesting has also been continued here since long ago and is still carried on by the Higashi Fuji Joint Use Cooperative. Of the 8,900ha. practice grounds, 6,000ha. are *kaya* fields, of which 200ha. within a 3,600ha. area are utilized. Harvesting takes place for about 50 days from December to February. 90% is hand-harvested using sickles. 30,000 medium-sized bundles of 2ft. circumference are obtained this way and about 20,000 bundles of 2~3ft. around are harvested by machine, for a total of about 50,000 bundles. The fields are burned off in the latter part of February. This is the largest *susuki* field in eastern Japan.

柄の長い鎌で手刈りする
Hand harvesting is done with a long-handled sickle.

茅葺き図鑑
Reference

手刈りしたものが上質の茅とされる。慣れた男性で1日に50〜60束、女性で40〜50束刈り取れる
Hand-harvested *kaya* is said to be of better quality. A man who is accustomed to the work can harvest 50~60 bundles a day, a woman 40~50 bundles.

結束機を使い、束の大きさを均一にそろえる
Kaya is bound securely in equal-sized bundles using a binding device.

茅場から富士山を望む
View of Mt. Fuji from the *kaya* field

77

富士山麓の茅場 The *Kaya* Fields at the Foot of Mt. Fuji

富士山の裾野に広がる茅場　　The *kaya* fields around the foot of Mt. Fuji

東富士演習場の初秋の茅場　　The *kaya* fields at the military practice area at Higashi Fuji

茅葺き図鑑
Reference

富士山を背景に茅刈り　　　Harvesting *kaya*, with Mt. Fuji in the background

北信州の茅葺き
Thatch in Northern Shinshu (Nagano Pref.)

白馬村沢渡集落 (2017)　　Sawawatari, Hakuba (2017)

北信州の茅葺き

北アルプス連峰の渓谷、糸魚川沿いに立地する小谷村、白馬村は、豪雪地帯である。豊富な森林資源を生かして豪雪に対処するための建ちの高い中二階造りの茅葺き民家が特徴的である。中二階や屋根裏では副業としての養蚕業を営み、生計を助けてきた。

この渓谷は、山国の信州と越後の海をつなぐ千国街道、別名塩の道とも呼ばれ、物資や人が往来する主要な街道であった。そのため、街道沿いの集落の民家は、はやくから中二階または二階建てとなっており、宿としての役割も果たしていた。

Thatch in Northern Shinshu

Otari and Hakuba villages are located in the snowy valley of the Northern Alps along the Itoi River. Plentiful forest resources have been utilized to build distinctive tall houses having a mezzanine floor and designed to cope with heavy snow. In the mezzanine floor and roof space, people raised silkworms to supplement their income.

This valley is the Chikuni Road, also known as the Salt Road, an important artery for the movement of goods and people between mountainous Shinshu and the Niigata seacoast. Because of this, houses in the villages along the road have long been built with a mezzanine or a second floor that served as lodging for travelers.

神城内山集落 (2017)
3棟の茅葺きの民家のほか、鉄板葺きも含めて茅葺き民家集落の景観をよくとどめている

Kamishiro Uchiyama village (2017)
With 3 thatched houses, as well as metal-covered thatched houses, this village retains the landscape of a village of thatched folk houses.

カリヤスの葺き替え（長野県小谷村、2018）
細くしなやかなカリヤスは緻密に屋根を葺くことができ、また雪に引き抜かれないために強く締め付けることができる
おしぼこには細くしなやかな雑木や根曲がり竹で茅をしっかりと押さえる

Rethatching with *kariyasu* (Otari, Nagano Pref., 2018)
With fine, pliant *kariyasu*, the roof can be thatched compactly and tied tightly so the *kaya* won't be pulled out by snow.
The *kaya* is held down tightly with sways of thin, pliant trees or bamboo.

二階建ての茅葺きの屋根裏は養蚕に使われていた様子をそのままとどめている。小屋組の下地には雑木が使われ、この地域の特徴を表す

The roof space of this two-story house remains as it was when it was used for raising silkworms. The use of miscellaneous trees for the truss is typical of this area.

千国街道
塩の道の牛方宿（長野県宝、2017）
Chikuni Road
Ushikata Juku on the Salt Road (Takara, Nagano Pref., 2017)

カリヤス

千国街道沿いの民家の茅葺き屋根の茅はカリヤスが一般的である。
カリヤスは標高の高い山地に適し、豪雪地帯では雪が降る前に刈ることができるカリヤスが使われてきた。カリヤスはススキに比べると丈も短く細いのでコガヤと呼ばれる。中空で撥水性がよく硬くて丈夫なので、この地域では50年以上持つ耐久性のある屋根を葺くことができる。
集落の背後の山にカリヤスの共有の茅場があり、その入会利用が今日まで続いている。カリヤスの茅場の維持管理と上質な茅を得るため、春には野火つけによる手入れも今日まで守られている。

Kariyasu

The thatched roofs of houses along the Chikuni Road are generally thatched using *kariyasu*, which is used because it is adapted to mountains at high elevations and can be harvested before the snow falls. Because *kariyasu* is shorter and thinner than *susuki*, it is called *kogaya*, meaning "little *kaya*." The stems are hollow, shed water well, and are strong, so in this area it is used to thatch roofs that can be expected to last more than 50 years.
There are communal fields of *kariyasu* in the mountains behind the villages, and joint use is still practiced. To maintain the fields and get high-quality *kaya* from them, they are burned off in the spring.

千国真木集落
南小谷の駅から歩いて1時間ほどの山間に残る茅葺き集落。およそ30年前に廃村となった村に、都市部からの移住者が住み継いだ。農業と自給的な共同生活を営んでいる。現在茅葺きの主屋が2棟のほか、板葺きが1棟、鉄板で覆われた茅葺きが3棟残されている

Chikuni Maki village
This village of thatched houses is in the mountains about an hour's walk from Minami Otari Station. The village was disbanded some thirty years ago, but has been kept up by people who have moved here from the city. They farm and have a self-sufficient communal way of life. At present, there are two thatched houses, one house roofed with wood, and three that have metal-covered thatch.

屋根は養蚕農家の特徴であり、この地域の特徴でもある前甲屋根となっている

The front helmet roof is the region's typical style, distinguishing a sericulture farm.

晴れた日は遠く北アルプスの山並みが望める
On a clear day, the Northern Alps range can be seen in the distance.

白馬山麓カリヤスの茅場 *Kariyasu* Fields at Mt. Hakuba (Nagano Pref.)

標高800〜1000mにある牧の入茅場
（ふるさと文化財の森　長野県小谷村、2015）

Makinoiri *kaya* field is at an elevation of 800~1,000 meters.
(Furusato Bunkazai no Mori, Otari, Nagano, 2015)

10月の刈り取り風景

Kariyasu harvest in October

茅葺き図鑑
Reference

腕に抱えながら鎌で刈る
The *kariyasu* is held with one arm and cut with a sickle.

茅で束ねる
Kariyasu is tied up with *kariyasu*.

刈った茅を6把ずつ立てて茅場で乾燥させる
Six bundles of cut *kariyasu* are stood together to dry in the field.

白馬山麓の中腹、標高800～1000mにカリヤスの茅場が広がる。集落の入会地として江戸時代から利用されてきた。そのうちのひとつ牧の入茅場は面積約6haで、刈り取り時期は10月20日前後の土用の日から山開きとなり、雪が降る11月中旬までの約20日間。刈り取った茅は茅場に立てて1週間～10日乾燥させて雪が積もる前11月中旬頃に搬出する。2尺〆の束で昔は12000把刈り取ることができたが、現在はススキが増え、カリヤスは5000～8000把の収穫量となっている。熟練者は1日120把、20立て分を刈り取って立てることができる。乾燥して搬出された茅は長さごとに選別して束ね直し、根元を押し切りで切り揃えて屋根葺き材料とする。雪がとけた4月末から5月初に野火つけを行い茅場を維持している。

Fields of *kariyasu* are spread on the slopes of Mt. Hakuba at an elevation of 800~1,000 meters. These fields have been used in common by the villagers since the Edo period (1603~1868). One of the fields is Makinoiri *kaya* field, an area of about 6ha., where the harvest begins around October 20 and continues for about 20 days until mid-November, when snow starts to fall. The harvested *kariyasu* is stood in the field to dry for a week to 10 days and carried out around the middle of November, before snow begins to settle. In the past, these fields provided 12,000 bundles 2 feet in circumference, but at present, *susuki* has made inroads and the *kariyasu* harvest is down to 5,000~8,000 bundles. An experienced person can harvest 120 bundles a day and divide it into 20 stacks. After being shipped out, the dried *kaya* is separated by length, rebundled, and trimmed with a straw cutter to even the root end and ready it for thatching. The *kaya* fields are maintained by burning them off in late April or early May, after the snow has melted.

白馬山麓カリヤスの茅場 *Kariyasu* Fields at Mt. Hakuba

牧の入茅場　　　　　　　　　　Makinoiri *kaya* field

茅葺き図鑑
Reference

野火つけ　　　　　　　　　　Burning off the field

五箇山の合掌造
Gokayama's *Gassho-zukuri* (Toyama Pref.)

主屋を6分割してその家でその年に刈った茅だけで屋根を葺く（富山県南砺市、1980）

The roof is divided into six sections and the owner thatches one section at a time using only the *kaya* harvested that year. (Nanto, Toyama Pref., 1980)

十数年という比較的短い周期で屋根を葺き替えるので、おろした古茅は再利用できる茅と傷んだ茅に分けて、傷んだ茅は回収して肥料として畑に施す（1980）

The roof is rethatched in a relatively short cycle of about a dozen years, so the old *kaya* is divided into that which is reusable and that which is damaged. The damaged *kaya* is retrieved and laid in the fields (1980).

相倉の茅場（富山県南砺市、2010）
標高が700m以上の急峻な斜面に茅場が設けられている
この急斜面はかつて焼畑として利用されていた跡を茅場に転用
したものと考えられる

Ai-no-Kura's thatch fields (Nanto, Toyama Pref., 2010)
The thatch beds are on steep slopes at an altitude of 700 meters or more.
It is believed that in the past, these steep slopes were used for slash-and-burn agriculture, after which they were turned into *kaya* fields.

五箇山の茅場

五箇山では各家で集落より高い急峻な山の中腹に2〜3反歩（2000〜3000㎡）のカリヤスの茅場を所有し、毎年茅刈りを行って屋根を維持してきた。菅沼集落では茅場が北斜面なので、刈ったカリヤスをすぐに集落に運び、合掌造の主屋や付属屋の軒下に立てかけ雪囲いとする。雪から建物を守るとともに、茅を翌春まで保存乾燥させる工夫である。その茅で翌春に屋根を葺き替えた。
一方、相倉集落では茅場が南面するので、刈った茅を地面に広げて1週間程乾燥した後、集落に運び、すぐ屋根を葺き替えることが一般的であった。

相倉集落の茅刈り（2011）
Ai-no-Kura's *kaya* harvest (2011)

刈った茅を地面に広げて1週間程乾燥する
The cut *kaya* is spread out on the ground to dry for about a week

Gokayama's *Kaya* Fields

In Gokayama, each household owns a *kariyasu* field of about 2,000~3,000m² high on the steep slopes of the mountains. The *kaya* is harvested every year to maintain the roofs. The Suganuma village *kaya* fields are on northern slopes, so the harvested *kariyasu* is taken to the village immediately and used for snow fences around houses and outbuildings. This protects the buildings from snow and dries and preserves the *kaya* until the following spring, when it is used to thatch the roofs.
On the other hand, Ai-no-Kura's *kaya* fields face south, so the cut *kaya* is spread out on the ground to dry for about a week, then taken to the village and, in the past, was generally used immediately to thatch the roofs.

相倉集落全景（世界文化遺産、富山県南砺市、2010）
Overview of Ai-no-Kura (World Heritage Site, Nanto, Toyama Pref., 2010)

相倉集落外観 (2013)　　　　　　　　　View of Ai-no-Kura (2013)

切妻の隅を丸く巻き込むように葺きおさめるのが五箇山の合掌造　The rounded barge is unique to Gokayama's *gassho-zukuri* (2013).
屋根の特徴である (2013)

相倉集落の冬の全景 (2012)　　　　　　　　　Overview of Ai-no-Kura in winter (2012)

根葺きまたは原始合掌造 (2013)
建設年代は不明であるが、これ自体がそれほど古いものではない。ただその形状や技術は遠く遡るという説があり合掌造の起源と考える説がある

"Root thatch" or primitive *gassho-zukuri* (2013)
Although it is unclear when this was built, it is not particularly old; but one theory has it that the shape and technique go far back and that it is the origin of *gasso-zukuri*.

相倉集落

越中富山の山中、庄川の上流の急峻な谷間に相倉集落は位置する。20棟の茅葺きを残す世界遺産合掌造集落のひとつである。大きな合掌造の茅葺き屋根が谷に沿うように同じ方向を向いて建ち並んでいる。

相倉には根葺き、股建、または原始合掌造と呼ばれる、三角形の屋根だけの建物が残されている。合掌造の成立にはもともとこのような切妻の素朴な屋根だけのものから合掌造に発達したという説と、下流域の富山県にあるような寄せ棟屋根から、破風を設けそれが拡大し、さらに最大限に屋根裏を拡大して切妻に至ったというふたつの説がある。

Ai-no-Kura Village

Ai-no-Kura is located in a steep valley in the mountains of Etchu Toyama on the upper reaches of the Sho River. With 20 thatched houses remaining, it is one of the World Heritage *gassho-zukuri* villages. The thatched roofs of the large *gassho-zukuri* are built facing the same direction, following the line of the valley.

In Ai-no-Kura stands a structure that is just a triangular roof. This is referred to as "root thatch," a "straddle structure," or a "primitive *gassho-zukuri*." One theory has it that *gassho-zukuri* developed from this kind of simple gabled structure with only a roof. Another theory is that the gables were first made on hipped roofs like those found in the area of Toyama downriver, thereby enlarging the space, and that eventually this was further enlarged to maximize roof space.

菅沼集落 (2013)

Suganuma village (2013)

菅沼集落の民俗資料館 (2012)
菅沼集落では茅場が北斜面で乾きにくいので、軒下に雪囲いとしてかきつけて翌春まで保存乾燥する
Suganuma Folk Museum (2012)
Because Suganuma's *kaya* fields are on northern slopes, the harvested *kaya* does not dry easily, so it is stored as snow fences around the houses, where it dries until the following spring.

菅沼集落

庄川の蛇行する河岸の内側台地に9棟の合掌造民家が、その曲がった川に沿うように立地している。これは合掌造の巨大な茅葺き屋根が横風に弱いため、川に沿って曲がる風向きにあわせてつくり、風に逆らわないよう合掌造を配置しているのである。

白川郷の合掌造がすべて切妻であるのに対して、五箇山の合掌造は切妻に茅葺きの庇がついた大きな入母屋造の屋根も少なくない。これは、合掌造の成立過程で、本来破風のない寄棟屋根から破風が設けられ、次第に切妻の合掌造に変わる過程のかたちとも考えられている。

Suganuma Village

Nine *gassho-zukuri* houses are located on a plateau on the inside of a bend in the Sho River, placed so they follow the curve of the river. The large *gassho-zukuri* are weak with respect to side winds, therefore the houses have been placed this way so as not to fight the wind that blows along the river bend.

Whereas the *gassho-zukuri* of Shirakawa-go all have simple gables, many of Gokayama's houses have a pent roof in front of the gable, creating large hipped and gabled roofs. This seems to have evolved in the process of development from an original hipped-roof style through the creation of a gable, eventually becoming the gabled style of the *gassho-zukuri*.

菅沼集落（世界文化遺産、富山県南砺市、2013）
蛇行する川に沿って合掌造の民家が配置されている
Suganuma village (World Heritage Site, Nanto Toyama Pref., 2013)
The *gassho-zukuri* houses are arranged following the bend in the river.

カリヤスの段階的利用　Stages in the Utilization of *Kariyasu*

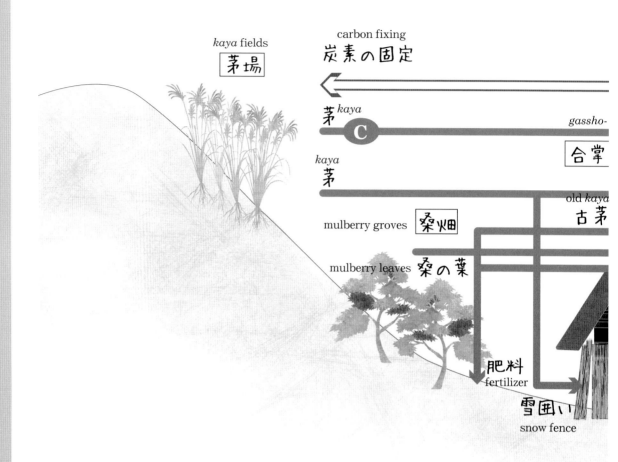

白川郷や五箇山の合掌造集落では、集落の背後の山の中腹、標高700〜1000mの高地に自生するカリヤスを茅として長年利用してきた。

カリヤスは10月中旬に枯れて刈り取ることができるので、雪の降る前に収穫できるという点でも茅として好都合であった。

秋に刈り取ったカリヤスは、里に運んで、その一部は家を守る雪囲いとなり、乾燥を兼ねて春まで保管される。春になると屋根に葺かれ、屋根からおろした古茅は、桑畑に施されて肥料となる。それが桑の萌芽を促進させ、蚕の生育を支える。合掌造集落は養蚕業が主産業であり、このカリヤスの段階的利用によって大きな合掌造の屋根を守るとともに、大量の蚕の生産が持続されてきたのである。

In the *gassho-zukuri* villages of Shirakawa-go and Gokayama, *kariyasu*, which is indigenous to the high elevations of 700~1,000 meters in the surrounding mountains, has long been utilized. *Kariyasu* is convenient because it withers in mid-October and thus can be harvested before the snow starts to fall.

Kariyasu harvested in autumn is taken to the villages, where part of it is used to make snow fences to protect the houses, in which form it dries out and is stored until spring. In the spring, it is used to thatch the roofs, and, in the past, old *kaya* from the roofs was put in the mulberry groves as fertilizer, thus promoting the germination of the mulberries, thereby supporting the raising of silkworms. Sericulture was the main industry of the *gassho-zukuri* villages, and the cycle of *kariyasu* use protected the roofs and, at the same time, made it possible to carry on silkworm production.

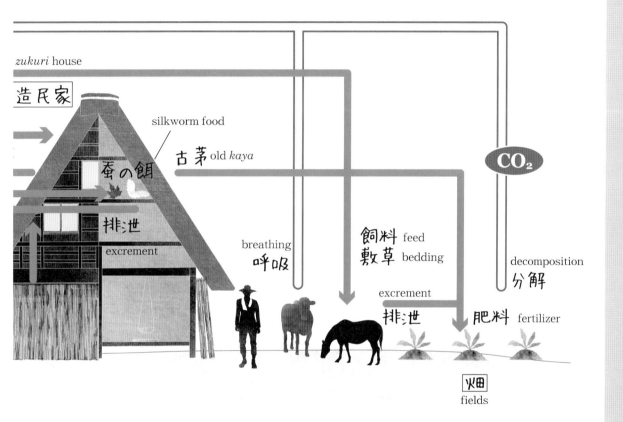

白川郷の合掌造
The *Gassho-zukuri* of Shirakawa-go (Gifu Pref.)

白川郷荻町合掌造民家集落（世界文化遺産、岐阜県白川村、1986）
谷沿いに棟を揃えて建ち並ぶ。合掌造は横からの風に弱いので、川に沿って吹きおりる風に対して妻側を向けて風を除けるように配置されたものである

The village of *gassho-zukuri* houses in Ogimachi, Shirakawa-go
(World Heritage Site; Shirakawa, Gifu Pref., 1986)
The ridges are lined up along the valley.
Because the roofs are weak with respect to side winds, the gable ends are placed facing the winds that blow down the river.

ユイの屋根葺き (1997)
荻町の全戸から男1人、まかないや下作業として女1人が参加して、共同で屋根葺きを行う

Thatching a roof with communal labor (1997)
Thatching in Ogimachi is done with communal labor. Each household supplies one man for thatching and one woman for cooking and ground support.

国指定重要文化財和田家住宅
白川郷で最も古く、最も大きな合掌造民家

The Wada House (Important Cultural Property)
This is the oldest and largest *gassho-zukuri* in Shirakawa-go.

白川郷の合掌造の屋根は切妻の端部が外側に転んで、棟が軒よりせり出して妻側を風雨から守るように工夫されている

The edges of the gables lean outwards on the *gassho-zukuri* of Shirakawa-go. Having the ridge jutting out protects the gable from wind and rain.

往時のようにツタで結んだ笄棟
飛騨民俗村　若山家住宅
棟際にミズハリと呼ばれる横木を茅葺き屋根を貫通させて取り付ける棟を葺き上げて棟積み茅を押さえる角材を固定するために、両側のミズハリからツタなどの縄を結んでしっかりと結び合わせる。
毎年春には、傷みの早い棟茅だけを積み直す必要があり、その際にこのミズハリからとった縄をはずすだけで容易に交換できるしくみでもある

A "skewered ridge" tied with vines as in the past
(The Wakayama House, Hida Folk Village; Takayama, Gifu Pref.)
Just below the ridge, the roof is pierced through by horizontal logs called *mizuhari*.
To secure the logs that hold down the *kaya* that is piled on the top of the roof, vines or ropes are laid across them and attached to the *mizuhari* on both sides of the roof.
Damaged ridge *kaya* must be replaced in the spring, a task which can be done easily by simply cutting the ropes.

合掌造の構造
合掌と呼ばれる三角形の構造で大きな茅葺き屋根と豪雪の重みを支える
その合掌材の根元はコマジリと呼ばれ、コマの芯のように尖らせて梁の上にのせてある。これによって、風や地震の力を受け流すしくみとなっている

The structure of the *gassho-zukuri*
The triangular brace structure, called "*gassho*," supports the weight of the large thatched roof and heavy snow.
The lower ends of the *gassho* braces are pointed and rest on the beams below, enabling them to parry the force of wind or earthquake.

白川郷には主屋の他に、穀物を乾燥し収蔵するハサ小屋がある。これは高床の倉であり、その周りにハサ木が渡され、穀物などの乾燥装置でもある。冬の早い白川郷で収穫した穀物の他に、屋根の茅であるカリヤスなどもこのハサ小屋で乾燥される

In addition to the main houses, Shirakawa-go also has sheds for drying and storing grain. These are raised-floor storehouses with racks around them for drying grain.
Winter comes early here, so thatch for the roof is also dried on these racks.

雪の合掌造集落（白川郷荻町）

Ogi, Shirakawa-go, in snow

白川郷の合掌造とその成立過程

白川郷の荻町には、80棟余りの合掌造の民家とハサ小屋などの付属屋をあわせると100棟を超す合掌造屋根がまとまって残されており、世界遺産に登録されている。

合掌造の特徴は、まず屋根が切妻であること。次に屋根の勾配が日本の一般的な茅葺き屋根の勾配が45度であるのに対して、合掌造の屋根は50度〜60度におよぶ急勾配となっており、屋根が高く、屋根裏空間が極めて大きいことである。妻側が大きく開く切妻屋根は、民家の屋根としては構造的にも不安定で、雨や風雪に対しても不利な点が多い。にもかかわらず、切妻屋根を採用しているのは、屋根裏で養蚕を行うためであると考えられる。

白川郷では、この茅葺きの切妻屋根は主屋だけではなく、ハサ小屋、便所など、付属屋の屋根も全て切妻となっている。また、五箇山では切妻屋根の端部の合掌組が垂直であるのに対して、白川郷ではそれが外側に転んで切妻屋根の雨仕舞に対する弱点を補っている。さらに、五箇山では切妻屋根の端部が丸く葺きおさめられているのに対して、白川郷では茅を斜めに葺いた切破風となっている。

以上のようなことから、白川郷では、元々切妻であったものが、養蚕農家としてより大きく急勾配に改造された。それに対して五箇山では、寄棟屋根から切妻へと変化が起きた。両者は相互に影響を受けながら違った発達過程を辿ったと考えられる。

The Process of Establishing Shirakawa-go's *Gassho-zukuri*

Shirakawa-go's Ogi-machi, which has been designated a World Heritage Site, has over 80 *gassho-zukuri* houses, which together with grain storehouses and other outbuildings, brings the total of *gassho-zukuri* structures to more than 100.

Gassho-zukuri are characterized first and foremost by the gabled roof. In addition, the roof slope is between 50 and 60 degrees, considerably steeper than the 45 degrees of thatched roofs in other parts of Japan. The roofs are high with very large roof spaces. The large opening on the gable end makes for an unstable roof structure, giving it many disadvantages with respect to rain and wind. The reason that this structure was adopted despite these problems seems to have been to allow for raising silkworms in the roof space.

In Shirakawa-go, not only the houses but all the outbuildings, as well, have the open gable. Whereas the roofs of Gokayama have a perpendicular gable, those of Shirakawa-go lean to the outside to offset the rain problem.

Moreover, whereas Gokayama's barges are thatched round, those in Shirakawa are thatched on a diagonal and cut off at the verge. From this it would seem that Shirakawa-go's roofs were originally gabled roofs that were restructured to a steep angle to make them larger for sericulture. Gokayama's roofs, on the other hand, changed from hipped and gabled roofs to gabled roofs. The two seem to have influenced each other, even while developing along different paths.

①屋根おろし
早朝薄暗い頃から家族と親戚で屋根の古茅をおろす
1) Removing the old roof
The family and relatives start removing the old *kaya* at the crack of dawn.

②下地の修理
雪の重みでずり落ちた垂木をネソ（マンサクの若木を叩いて繊維状によじったもの）で結び直す
2) Repairing the frame
Rafters that have been dislodged by the weight of the snow are retied using *neso* (the young branches of hazel that have been beaten to loosen the fibers, then twisted).

③軒付け　茅束を軒に1束ずつしっかり結び付けていく
3) Starting the eaves
Bunches of *kaya* are firmly secured to the eaves one at a time.

④カタキリ
切妻の端はカタキリと呼ばれに斜めに葺いて雨仕舞をする難しい技なので、ベテランが担当して平葺きに先行して葺き上げる
4) *Katakiri*
The gable uses a difficult technique that involves thatching on the diagonal (*katakiri*). A veteran thatcher handles this and thatches up the side ahead of the roof plane.

⑤平葺き
軒付けとカタキリにあわせて、長い茅をそのまま並べて葺き上げる 茅にマンサクのおしぼこを押しあて、針で刺し通して屋根裏の下地から縄をとり、カケヤでおしぼこを叩いてしっかりと締める
5) Thatching the roof plane
As the gable is being thatched, long *kaya* is laid along the roof plane. Sways are laid on this and rope pushed with a needle to the underside, where it is wrapped around the frame and returned to the top. The sways are beaten with a mallet so the ropes can be tied tightly.

⑥棟仕舞
棟まで茅が葺き上がると、棟にへの字に茅を積み上げてそれを角材で押さえミズハリから縄をとって結ぶ
6) Finishing the ridge
When the roof has been thatched to the top, *kaya* is piled on the ridge in an inverted V shape; this is held down with logs that are tied down with rope attached to the *mizuhari*.

⑦朝から葺いて夕方までには葺き上がる
7) The job starts in the morning and is finished by evening.

白川郷のユイ (1981)　　　　Communal thatching in Shirakawa-go (1981)

⑧マエビルとコビル
朝早くからの手伝いに対して昼食と午前と午後それぞれ1回ずつの休憩に、当家からのご馳走がふるまわれて労がねぎらわれる
葺き上がった夕方には直会が設けられ、酒と踊りで皆が喜びを分かち合う

8) Feeding the participants
For the people who have been helping since early morning, the owner of the house provides lunch and morning and afternoon snacks to reward them for their efforts.
In the evening, after the roof is finished, a party is held where everyone can celebrate the completion of the new roof with drink and dancing.

白川郷のユイと茅頼母子

白川郷の屋根の葺き替えはユイと呼ばれる集落の相互扶助で行われる。五箇山では屋根を分割して少人数で葺き替えることが可能であるのに対して、白川郷では巨大な合掌屋根の片面を集落総出の大人数で1日で葺き上げる。

そのユイでは、各家が互いに屋根葺きの労働の貸し借りを平等に行うしくみが厳格に守られる。また、それに必要な茅は、各家で毎年刈り取った茅を持ち寄り、茅の貸し借りを行う頼母子講によって大量の茅を集めることが可能であった。

毎年春雪がとける頃に行われる、この壮大な屋根葺きの行事は、集落総出のお祭りのような性格を持ち、山深い豪雪地帯で暮らす人々の絆を強く結ぶ役割もあったのである。

Communal Labor and Sharing *Kaya* in Shirakawa-go

Roofs in Shirakawa-go are thatched under a system of mutual help called *yui*. In Gokayama, because the roofs are divided into sections, it is possible to thatch with few people. In Shirakawa-go, however, one entire side of the huge *gassho* roof is thatched in a day with the help of the entire village. Under this system, the equal borrowing and lending of labor is strictly observed. In the past, the enormous amount of *kaya* necessary was secured through a system for borrowing and lending the *kaya* that each family harvested every year.

This huge thatching event, held each spring when the snow thaws, is like a festival involving the entire village and has also functioned to strengthen ties among the people who live in this snowy village deep in the mountains.

琵琶湖のヨシ原 The *Yoshi* (Reed) Beds of Lake Biwa (Shiga Pref.)

水辺のヨシ原（滋賀県安土町下豊浦、2014）　Reed beds at the lakeside (Shimotoira, Azuchi, Shiga Pref., 2014)

ヨシ刈りのようす（2002）　Harvesting *yoshi* (2002)

茅葺き図鑑
Reference

刈り取られたヨシは色、太さ、長さによって細かく選別される（2002）

The harvested *yoshi* is separated into several categories by thickness and length (2002).

ヨシで葺かれた屋根
国指定重要文化財辻家住宅（滋賀県長浜市、2014）
A reed-thatched roof
The Tsuji House (Important Cultural Property; Nagahama, Shiga Pref., 2014)

琵琶湖の湖岸や内湖の周辺にヨシ原が広がる。昭和20年代には約260haあったヨシ原が、一時は半分の約130haに減少し、滋賀県によって琵琶湖ヨシ群落保全条例が定められるなどしてヨシ原の保全と再生がなされ、現在では約170haに回復している。古くは安土桃山時代からヨシ製品が生産され、江戸時代からヨシが生産され商いされるようになった。刈り取り時期は1月〜3月。屋根材として使われるほかに、ヨシズやスダレや建具や天井材など、高級建材としても利用されている。3月末に野焼きが行われる。

Yoshi beds are spread along the banks of Lake Biwa and its canals. In 1940, there were about 260ha. of reed beds, but at one point, their area had shrunk to around 130ha., half that amount. Under the Shiga Ordinance for the Conservation of Reed Vegetation Zones, the reed beds are now protected and have recovered to the extent of about 170ha. In the Azuchi-Momoyama period (1573~1603), *yoshi* products were manufactured, and in the Edo Period (1603~1868), *yoshi* was grown for the market. The reed is harvested from January thru March. In addition to being used as thatch, *yoshi* is utilized as a high-quality building material for interior furnishings such as mats, screens, and ceilings. The reed beds are burned off at the end of March.

琵琶湖のヨシ原 The *Yoshi* (Reed) Beds of Lake Biwa

最も上質なヨシを産出してきたといわれる内湖西の湖のヨシ地（2002）

茅葺き図鑑
Reference

The reed beds at Nishinoko on the southeast shore of Lake Biwa are reputed to produce the highest quality *yoshi* (2002).

美山町北集落
Kita Village in Miyama (Kyoto Pref.)

美山町北集落全景（重要伝統的建造物群保存地区、2010）　約40棟の入母屋屋根の茅葺き民家が山裾に寄り添っている

View of Kita village in Miyama (Important Preservation District for Groups of Traditional Buildings; 2010)
About 40 hipped and gabled thatched houses nestle at the foot of the hills.

入母屋屋根の破風が建ち並ぶ (2010)

The lined-up gables of hipped and gabled roofs (2010)

棟はクリの置千木 (2010)
その上にのるユキワリは根曲りのスギ丸太
The ridge is finished with chestnut *chigi* (2010).
Over the *chigi* is laid a curved cedar log.

屋根を前、後ろ、両側の四分割にして順番に葺き替えていく
棟は前を葺き替えるときに合わせて葺くのが一般的である
（1980）

The roof is divided into 4 parts, front, back, and two sides, which are rethatched in turn.
The ridge is usually rethatched when the front of the roof is thatched (1980).

破風には意匠が凝らされる (2010)
Designs on the gables (2010)

美山町北集落

京都府南丹市美山町には今日でも300棟余りの茅葺き民家が残され、西日本有数の茅葺き民家集落である。その中で北集落は40棟余りの茅葺き民家を残し、国の重要伝統的建造物群保存地区に指定されている。

里山を背後に手前に川が流れ、その山裾に集落がまとまる景観は、西日本の特徴的な農村集落の姿を今日によくとどめている。集落の背後には茅場があり、各家で1反歩（1000㎡）程度の茅場を所有して、毎年茅を刈って蓄え屋根をいくつかに分割して葺き替えてきた。茅葺きは入母屋造の屋根が基本で、周囲に杉皮葺きなどの下屋がまわるかたちが一般的である。

入母屋の破風には板をくり抜いて家紋の装飾が施され、端正で美しい茅葺きの景観を際立たせている。

近年日本の茅葺き民家が衰退し、職人の数も激減する中で、美山の茅葺きは最後まで踏みとどまり、若手の職人も育成されて、今日の日本の茅葺き文化復活の起点ともなっている。

Kita Village in Miyama, Kyoto

Even now, over 300 thatched houses are left in Miyama, Nantan, Kyoto, making it one of western Japan's most outstanding villages of thatched houses. Kita has over 40 thatched houses and has been designated an Important Preservation District for Groups of Traditional Buildings. This village retains the characteristic appearance of rural villages in western Japan, nestled against the local hills with a river in front. Each household owns about 1,000m² of *kaya* fields at the rear of the village and harvests the *kaya* annually, saving it up to thatch portions of the roof as maintenance demands. The thatched roof is basically hip-and-gable style, but it is common to have a lower roof, thatched with cedar bark, around the central thatched roof.

A board carved with the family crest decorates the barge of the hipped and gabled roof, accenting the lovely thatched landscape.

In recent years, the number of thatched houses in Japan has declined, and the number of thatchers has fallen drastically, but thatching in Miyama has held its ground, and young thatchers are being trained, making this the starting point for the revival of thatching culture in Japan today.

集落背後の山から集落を望む (2010)   A view of the village from the mountains behind it (2010)

東播磨の茅葺き
The Thatched Houses of Higashi Harima (Hyogo Pref.)

針目覆の棟の民家（兵庫県神戸市、1994）
東播磨の茅葺き民家の棟は、千木と針目覆と二種類見られる。
山裾には千木が多く、平野部には針目覆が多い

House with a *harime-oi* ridge (Kobe, Hyogo Pref., 1994)
The thatched houses of Higashi Harima have two ridge styles, *chigi* and *harime-oi*.
Chigi are common at the foot of the mountains, while *harime-oi* are more common on the plains.

入母屋で針目覆の主屋と書院（1994）

Hipped and gabled main and guest houses with *harime-oi* (1994)

箱木千年家(国指定重要文化財　15世紀　兵庫県神戸市北区)
主屋と書院が鉤の手に並ぶ。
15世紀は戦国時代でその世相を反映して土壁で囲われた閉鎖的な構え

The Hakogi Sennen House (Important Cultural Property; 15th century, Kobe, Hyogo Pref.)
The main house and guest house form an L shape.
Reflecting the conditions of civil war in the 15th century, the property is enclosed with an earthen wall.

東播磨の茅葺き

大都市神戸の北側六甲山の背後に豊かな農村地帯が広がり、数百棟の茅葺き民家が現存している。集落としてのまとまりはないが、里山を背景に田畑の中に茅葺きの民家が点在している。この一帯、東播磨地方は、大都市に近い立地から、稲作のほかにも多様な園芸作物に恵まれ、農家の経営が安定する中で、主屋のほかにも書院や納屋も茅葺きとして残された例も少なくない。
その中に現存する日本最古の民家で15世紀に遡るとされる箱木千年家も移築保存され、往時の民家のつくりの特徴を今日に伝えている。

The Thatched Houses of Higashi Harima

Behind the Rokko Mountains to the north of the metropolis of Kobe, in the area known as Higashi Harima, there are several hundred thatched houses. They do not form a single village, but are dotted across the rural landscape against a backdrop of local hills. Being located near a large city, rural households have stable income from rice and a wide variety of horticultural products, and thatched roofs can be found not only on many houses but also on guest houses and barns.
Among them is Japan's oldest surviving house, the Hakogi Sennen House, which dates back to the 15th century. It has been moved here and preserved, enabling us to see the characteristics of houses of the time.

針目覆の棟と竹の根を生かしたカラスドマリ
Ridge with *harime-oi* and bamboo-root "crow's perch"

田植えの頃の水田に映る茅葺き民家 （神戸市北区淡河町、1994）

Thatched house reflected in a rice paddy around planting time (Ogo, Kobe, 1994)

左が書院で右が妻入りの主屋（兵庫県三木市、1994）

On the left, a guest house; on the right, a house with the entrance on the gable end (Miki, Hyogo Pref., 1994)

妻入りの入母屋の破風には家の正面としての装飾が施され、千木と一体となった端正な佇まい（1994）

Above the entrance to the house, the gable bears a decoration that blends well with the *chigi* (1994).

田んぼにうど小屋が数棟建ち並び、晩秋の風物詩でもある
（兵庫県三田市、2008）

In autumn, udo sheds stand in the rice paddies (Sanda, Hyogo Pref., 2008).

苫を下から葺き重ねて最後に棟にワラ束を被せて棟仕舞をする

Rush mats are laid on the shed from the bottom up and bundles of rice straw finish off the ridge.

棟の稲ワラを棒で差し上げる

Rice straw is handed up to the ridge with a pole.

苫は穂先を下に向けた逆葺きとして葺き重ね、数年ごとに更新されていく

The mats are made with the tops of the straw hanging down and are replaced every few years.

苫は丸めて納屋に収納保管される

The mats are rolled up and stored in the barn.

うど小屋

兵庫県三田市では特産のうどの促成栽培が盛んである。秋に収穫を終えたあとの田んぼに小屋をつくり、その中にうどを植え込み、ワラを積み上げその発酵熱で栽培を促す。小屋はスギの丸太で三角形に組んだ構造に、あらかじめ稲ワラを編んで筵状にした苫をつくり、穂先を下に向けた逆葺きとして、下から順に葺き重ねていく。春にうどの収穫が終わると、小屋は解体され苫は丸めて保管されて数年間再利用される。ワラを生かした昔ながらの素晴らしい知恵は、今でも最高品質のウドの生産を支えている。

Udo Sheds

For the forced cultivation of udo, a specialty of the area, udo is planted in the rice paddies after the autumn harvest. Rice straw is piled over it, employing the heat of fermentation to promote growth. Over this, triangular sheds are made using cedar logs, over which mats of woven rice straw are hung from bottom to top, with the tops of the straw hanging down. After the spring udo harvest, the sheds are dismantled and the mats stored for reuse for a few more years. This clever device, long practiced to make good use of rice straw, is still used to produce high-quality udo.

出雲平野の反り棟
The Curved Roofs of the Izumo Plain (Shimane Pref.)

斐伊川と出雲平野の散居村（2007）

The scattered houses of a village on the Hii River and the Izumo plain (2007)

北西部に築地松が四角に刈りそろえられる。
この築地松は毎年のように剪定され、その枝が燃料として日々の暮らしを支えた（2007）

On the northwest side, the dike pines have been trimmed into a box shape.
The dike pines were trimmed every year and their branches served as fuel to support daily life (2007).

大きく反り上がった棟が入母屋屋根のかたちを見せる (2007)

The high curve of the ridge accents the shape of the hipped and gabled roof (2007).

反り棟は茅を端部に積み上げて、竹で巻いてかたちづくられる (2007)

The shape of the curve is created by piling *kaya* at the ends of the ridge and wrapping it with bamboo (2007).

棟の端部に茅を高く積み上げて反り棟をかたちづくる
(島根県出雲市、2016)

Kaya is piled high on the ridge ends to form the curved ridge
(Izumo, Shimane Pref., 2016).

竹を巻いて棟仕舞をする(2016)

The ridge is finished off with a bamboo wrapping (2016).

出雲平野の反り棟

出雲平野は中国山地から流れ出る斐伊川の河口に形成された平野である。古代よりタタラ製鉄によって出雲の山中では森林の伐採と砂鉄の採集によって山が切り崩され、大雨のたびに洪水が頻発した。その長年の土砂の堆積によってつくられたのが出雲平野である。肥沃な土地ではあるが、たびたび川の氾濫に悩まされてきたので、屋敷の周りを築地で囲い、松を植林して洪水から守ってきた。

屋敷は平野全域に散居し、築地松を洪水への備えとするほかに冬の季節風からの風よけとして、また、その枝葉を燃料として活用するという散居村特有の景観が形成された。茅葺きの民家は、刈り揃えられた築地松の上に棟だけが顔をのぞかせ、そこが茅葺き屋根であることがうかがえる。その棟が遠景からも際立つように反り上がり、同じく端部が反り上がって剪定された築地松と相まって、端正で雄大な農村景観をつくりあげている。茅葺き屋根の形式としては寄棟屋根であるが、反り上がった棟の端は入母屋屋根のようにかたちづくられる。築地松の上にひときわ高く見える反り棟は、風雪にさらされてもなお力強く茅葺き屋根を守っているのである。

The Curved Roofs of the Izumo Plain

The Izumo plain is formed at the mouth of the Hii River, which flows from the Chugoku mountains. In ancient times, the forests of the Izumo mountains were cut down and the mountain sides excavated to collect iron sand for manufacturing iron, causing flooding with every heavy rain. Over the centuries, the resulting accumulation of earth and sand created the Izumo plain. The land is fertile, but because the river frequently flooded the area, residences were surrounded with dikes planted with pine trees. These houses are scattered throughout the plain. In addition to flood protection, the pine groves protect the properties from the wind and have provided wood for fuel, creating a landscape typical of such scattered villages. The ridges of thatched roofs peek out from above the carefully trimmed pines. To make the roofs stand out from a distance, the ridges are curved, and the pine groves are also trimmed to form a curve with high ends, creating a lovely, broad rural landscape. The roofs are hipped, but the ends of the curved ridge create the appearance of a hip-and-gable roof. The curved roof appearing above the dike pines protects the thatched roof even in the face of wind and snow.

箱棟となった茅葺き民家
反り棟を維持することが困難になり瓦葺きの箱棟に変わる家が多い
（2007）

This thatched house was changed to a box ridge.
Many houses have changed to tile-covered box ridges because of the difficulty of maintaining the curved ridge (2007).

箱棟を茅葺き屋根より高く突き上げてつくり、反り棟の姿を継承している（2007）

The shape of the curved ridge is maintained by elevating the box ridge high above the thatched roof (2007).

出雲平野の東部に隣接する地域の棟仕舞
棟の反りは出雲平野に比べるとゆるやかである (2007)

The ridge of a house in an area to the east of the Izumo plain
The ridge curve is gentler than those found on the Izumo plain (2007).

鳥取県福田家住宅の針目覆の棟仕舞（国指定重要文化財、鳥取県鳥取市、2007）

Harime-oi on the Fukuda House (Important Cultural Property; Tottori, Tottori Pref., 2007)

四国の茶堂　Shikoku's Tea Pavilions

下遊子茶堂（愛媛県西予市城川町遊子谷）
集落の入り口の見晴らしのよいがけ上に建つ茶堂。棟は箱棟となっている

Shimoyusu Tea Pavilion (Yusutani, Shirokawa-cho, Seiyo, Ehime Pref.)
This box-ridged pavilion is situated on a cliff at the village entrance, giving it a good view.

茶や谷茶堂（高知県高岡郡梼原町茶や谷）
集落の中心、道の分かれ道に建つ石仏と茶堂。奥には弘法大師が祀られている。入母屋屋根に針目覆の棟

Chayadani Pavilion (Chayadani, Yusuhara-cho, Takaoka-gun, Kochi Pref.)
A stone Buddha and a tea pavilion stand at a crossroads in the center of the village. To the rear, Kobo Daishi is honored. The hipped and gabled roof has a *harime-oi* ridge.

茅葺き図鑑
Reference

西上茶堂（愛媛県西予市野村町惣川）
山頂の見晴らしのよい場所に建つ茶堂
方形の屋根に棟茅を高く積みその頂部に甕を被せて棟
をおさめる
Nishiue Tea Pavilion (Sogawa, Nomura-cho, Seiyo, Ehime Pref.)
This pavilion stands at the top of a mountain, giving it a good view. The square roof has the ridge *kaya* piled high and covered with an earthenware pot.

小屋町茶堂（愛媛県西予市城川町窪野）
方形の屋根頂部を杉皮で巻きその頂部を縛っておさめている
Koyamachi Pavilion (Kubono, Shirokawa-cho, Seiyo, Ehime Pref.)
The top of this square roof is covered with cedar bark and finished off by tying the top.

茶や谷茶堂内部
Interior of Chaya-dani Tea Pavilion

茶堂は集落住民が共有するもので、木像、石仏などを安置して諸仏を祀り、津野公の霊を慰め、行路の人々に茶菓の接待を地区民が輪番で行い、信仰と心情と社交の場として、役割を果たしてきた。この茶堂は、高知県の西部山間部と愛媛県の西南部に広く分布し、数百棟という多くの茶堂が今日にも残されている。集落の入り口や交差点、見晴らしのいい場所などに建っている。四本柱で支えられた4畳半程度の壁のない屋根だけの四阿である。高床の床が張られ、奥には弘法大師が祀られていることが多い。この弘法大師ゆかりの四国八十八ヵ所巡りのお遍路さんの休息所としても使われている。

Tea pavilions are the common property of a village. Wooden or stone Buddhist statues may be placed in them, often to pacify the spirit of Chikatada Tsuno, an historical figure who was murdered in 1600, and villagers take turns at offering tea and sweets to passersby, making the pavilions places for devotion and socializing. Several hundred of these tea pavilions still stand, widely distributed in the mountains of western Kochi and southwestern Ehime prefectures. They stand in scenic spots at village entrances or at crossroads. They consist of just a roof supported by four posts over a raised floor of about four tatami mat size, with no walls. To the rear, they often have statues of the Buddhist priest Kobo Daishi (Kukai; 774~835). They serve as resting places for the pilgrims who journey around Shikoku's 88 temples, which are associated with Kobo Daishi.

筑後川流域の杉皮葺き
Cedar-Bark Thatch in the Chikugo River Basin (Fukuoka Pref.)

茅と杉皮の重ね葺き集落（重要伝統的建造物群保存地区　福岡県うきは市新川、1988）

A village of houses thatched with cedar bark over *kaya* (Important Preservation District for Groups of Traditional Buildings; Niikawa, Ukiha, Fukuoka Pref., 1988)

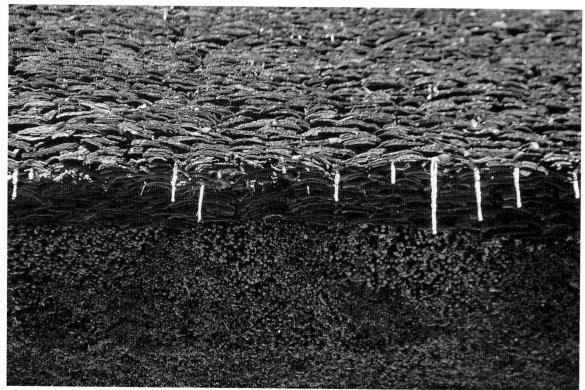

茅葺き屋根の上にスギの切り皮を15cm程度葺き重ねてある

Cut cedar bark has been laid on this thatched roof to a depth of about 15 centimeters.

隅は特に流れが緩いので、上質な杉皮や檜皮を葺き重ねて補強される

The slope on the corner is particularly gradual, so it is reinforced with layers of high-grade cedar and cypress bark.

材料となるスギの切り皮の束
製材所に頼んで分けてもらい、切り揃えて屋根に葺く

Bundles of cut cedar bark for thatching
The bark is procured from lumber mills, then cut into shape to thatch the roof.

筑後川流域の杉皮葺き

筑後川流域は温暖多雨な気候で森林資源に恵まれ、山間の農村集落でも棚田を築いて集約的な農林業が営まれてきた。里山には茅場も確保され、ススキで屋根が葺かれてきたが、昭和初期の戦争の時代になると、スギの植林が奨励され、この筑後川上流域は日本有数の林業地帯に生まれ変わった。その結果、茅場にも植林が進み、茅が不足する中で、増産された小麦のワラで屋根を葺いて一時的に凌いだ。それからさらに、豊富なスギの製材から生じる杉皮を茅葺き屋根に葺き被せる屋根が生まれたのである。スギは秋から春にかけて伐採されるが、その間、杉皮は剥ぎにくく、幅広い皮をむくことは難しいので、細く裂いた切り皮を茅のように敷き並べて、あたかも茅葺きのような姿に葺き替えたのである。この杉皮葺きは雨に強く、表面に苔が生えても傷まず、耐久性もあり、そして風流な屋根として筑後川下流域にも広がることになった。

今日、スギの造林は大きな蓄積を増し、そのスギの活用が求められる中で、副産物としての豊富な杉皮の活用策も模索されている。この杉皮で葺いた茅葺き屋根は、これからの日本の茅葺きの新たな資材としての杉皮の大きな可能性を示すものでもある。

Cedar-Bark Thatch in the Chikugo River Basin

With its warm, rainy climate, the Chikugo River basin is rich in forest resources. Rural villages in the mountains built terraced rice paddies and have practiced intensive agriculture and forestry. They had *kaya* fields in the local mountains and thatched with *susuki*, but during the war period, planting cedar was promoted, turning the upper Chikugo River area into one of Japan's main forestry regions. In consequence, forests supplanted the *kaya* fields, leading to a shortage of *kaya* that was temporarily gotten through by using the increased supply of wheat straw for thatch. Subsequently, the abundant supply of cedar bark from the lumber mills came to be used to cover the thatched roofs. Cedar is cut from autumn until spring, but during this season it is difficult to peel the bark in wide strips, so narrow strips of bark were cut and laid on the roof the same way as *kaya*, making the roof look as if it had been rethatched with *kaya*. This cedar bark repels rain and is durable, even when the surface is covered with moss, so it became fashionable for roofs in the lower reaches of the Chikugo River, as well.

Today the area has a large store of planted cedar trees that need to be put to use, and uses for the plentiful cedar bark are also being explored. These roofs thatched with cedar bark are suggestive of the great potential for cedar bark to become a new thatching material in Japan in the future.

杉皮で葺かれる前は、茅の針目覆の棟仕舞であったが、杉皮で葺かれるようになると、杉皮と千木で棟をおさめるようになり、その両者が融合された棟仕舞も見られる

Before roofs were thatched with cedar bark, the ridge was finished off with *harime-oi* using *kaya*, but after cedar bark came into use, the ridge was finished with cedar bark and *chigi*. Sometimes the two methods are mixed.

茅の上に杉皮を葺き重ねた民家全景（1988）
うまやが鍵形に主屋に接続されている

View of a house thatched with cedar bark over *kaya* (1988)
The stable is connected to the house in an L shape.

新たな里山となったスギの人工林を背景に、新たな茅葺きとしての茅の上に杉皮を葺き重ねた屋根

Against the backdrop of the planted cedar forests that have become the new vegetation of the local hills, roofs covered with cedar bark over *kaya* have become a new form of thatch.

数年経つと杉皮の表面は緑の苔に覆われ、風情のある姿に変わっていく

After a few years, the surface of the cedar bark acquires an attractive covering of moss.

佐賀のくど造
The *Kudo-zukuri* of Saga Pref.

くど造集落（佐賀県鹿島市犬王袋、2002）
ひときわ高いのは寿福院

A village of *kudo-zukuri* (Inuofukuro, Kashima, Saga Pref., 2002)
The especially high roof is a temple.

鍵形のくど造民家

An L-shaped *kudo-zukuri* house

コの字形のくど造民家の表
The front of a C-shaped *kudo-zukuri* house

コの字形のくど造民家の裏
谷は瓦葺きの下屋でつながれ内部は一体化されている
The back of a C-shaped *kudo-zukuri* house
The interior is unified with a lower tiled roof in the "valley."

山口家住宅（国指定重要文化財　佐賀県川副町、2002）
ロの字形のくど造民家

The Yamaguchi House (Important Cultural Property; Kawasoe, Saga Pref., 2002)
A square-shaped *kudo-zukuri* house

硬いヨシの特性を生かして隅を反り上げる

The stiffness of the reed is utilized to give the corners an upward slant.

棟の妻正面　ミンノスと呼ばれる牛の顔と耳を表している

The front of this gable depicts the face and ears of a cow.

口の字形の屋根中央部はじょうご形の谷となり、雨水をそこに集めて大きな瓦の樋で外に流す

The center of a square-shaped *kudo-zukuri* forms a funnel where rain water is collected and drained to the outside through a large tile trough.

佐賀平野のヨシ原（2002）
湿地にヨシが生え、そのヨシを刈り取って積み上げて農地をつくり、それを繰り返して干拓が拡大されていった

Reed beds of the Saga plain (2002)
The reeds growing in the wetlands were cut down and piled up to create farmland, a process that was repeated to expand the drained area.

佐賀平野のクリーク
湿地の排水を促すため、縦横にクリークが廻らされる
毎年そのクリークに生えるヨシや底に溜まる土砂をさらって肥料とし、クリークを維持した

Creeks on the Saga plain
To promote drainage of the wetland, creeks were created crisscrossing the area.
Every year the reeds growing in the creeks and the soil that collected in them were taken out to use as fertilizer, thereby maintaining the creeks.

山口家住宅（国指定重要文化財　佐賀県川副町）
ロの字形の平面でじょうごのような屋根に集まる雨水を外に排出するために、大きな樋が外に貫通している

The Yamaguchi House (Important Cultural Property; Kawasoe, Saga Pref.)
In a house with a square floorplan, the roof acts like a funnel collecting rainwater, which is discharged through an enormous trough that goes through to the outside.

佐賀平野は粘土質の土質を生かした焼き物が盛んであり、大きな瓦、がんぶり瓦をのせて棟をおさめる
Taking advantage of the clay soil of the Saga plain, much pottery is produced, and huge tiles are made to cover the roof ridge.

じょうごのような屋根の内部と雨水を外に流すための大きな樋
The interior of the funnel-like roof and the large trough for discharging rainwater

くど造の成立過程
The process of establishing the kudo-zukuri

鍵形　L shape　　　　コの字形　C shape　　　　ロの字形　closed square shape

佐賀のくど造

佐賀平野は有明海北部に広がる低湿地帯を干拓してつくられた豊かな農村地帯であり、くど造と呼ばれる独自な民家形式が発達している。くど造は鍵形に曲がった形式が「くど」すなわち「かまど」のようなかたちをしているので、そう呼ばれる。このくど造は、鍵形から、コの字形、ロの字形へと多様な平面形に発達し、特にロの字形は、屋根の谷が中央部に集まり、その雨水を大きな樋で外側に排出するというまことに不思議なつくりとなっている。佐賀藩では、干拓された広大な平野に木材資源が乏しいので、民家をつくる上で、梁間を2間に規制してきた。民家は2間の梁間を守りながらもより広い家をつくろうとした結果、鍵形からコの字型、ロの字形へと発達していったと考えられる。その結果、面積が広い割には、屋根が低く、風圧を受けにくいつくりとなって、台風に対しても守りやすいかたちとなったという利点もあったので、くど造は佐賀平野全域に普及していったのである。

佐賀平野は干拓を繰り返して拡大され、次第に豊かな農業生産を得ることになった。民家もはじめは小さく簡素な鍵形であったものから、その農地の拡大によって経営が豊かになり、それに応じて民家にもこのような独自の発達拡大の過程が生まれたのであろう。

The *Kudo-zukuri* of Saga Pref.

The Saga plain is an area of rich farmland created by draining the low wetlands at the north of the Ariake Sea. A unique type of house called *kudo-zukuri* developed here. The name derives from the L shape reminiscent of a cooking hearth. The *kudo-zukuri* evolved from an L shape to a C shape, and then to a closed square shape, so a wide variety of floorplans can be found. An especially unusual contrivance is the way rain that collects in the valley created by roofs of the square-shaped houses is carried out of the house by a large trough. Because the large plain that was created by draining is poor in timber resources, the width of houses was limited to about 180cm. The houses seem to have evolved from the L shape to the C shape and closed square shape in an effort to create a larger house while obeying this rule. As a result, relative to area, the roofs are low, so less susceptible to wind pressure, therefore easier to protect from typhoons, because of which they spread throughout the Saga plain.

The Saga plain was repeatedly enlarged through draining, gradually resulting in prosperous agriculture. The houses, too, were initially small, simple L shapes, but as farmers grew wealthier, the houses also underwent a unique process of development and enlargement.

阿蘇の茅場　The *Kaya* Fields at Mt. Aso (Kumamoto Pref.)

阿蘇外輪山に広がる草原　大きなカルデラ地形　麓に集落がある
The grasslands spread across the mountains around the giant caldera　Villages are situated below the mountains.

阿蘇の採草地の野焼き
早春に全ての採草地が野焼きされ、ススキの芽吹きを促す
Burning the grasslands at Mt. Aso
All the *kaya* fields are burned off in early spring, promoting the growth of new *susuki*.

茅葺き図鑑
Reference

採草地
平坦地は牛馬の飼料や農業資材用に大型機械で採草し、斜面地は茅として鎌で刈る

Meadows
On level ground, the grass is harvested with large farm machines to use for livestock feed; on the slopes, it is harvested with sickles to use as *kaya*.

茅は鎌で丁寧に刈りとる
Kaya is carefully harvested by hand with sickles.

根元を突きそろえて束ねる
The ends are butted to even them before binding.

草千里とも呼ばれる阿蘇外輪山に広がる日本最大の草原。約22000haの草原があり、うちススキの草原が約15000ha。標高はおよそ900m。阿蘇の草原のほとんどは集落ごとに定められた入会地となっており、牧野組合によって管理されている。刈り取り時期は12月末から4月上旬で、3月初旬頃から新芽が出ないうちに1ヶ月ほどかけて順次野焼きをしている。2尺〆で約2万束以上が収穫される。鎌の手刈りが主で、慣れた男性で1日に60〜70束刈り取ることができる。昭和30年代頃までは、麓の集落から外輪山の採草地への行き来に時間がかかるため、採草地に竹の骨組みと茅でつくった草泊まりをつくり、10日程度そこに泊まって採草を行っていた。

Japan's largest grassland is Kusasenri, which spreads across the mountains surrounding the Mt. Aso caldera. There are about 22,000ha. of which 15,000ha. are *susuki* grasslands, at an elevation of 900 meters. Most of the Aso grasslands are set as the communal property of villages and are managed by pastureland cooperatives. The *kaya* harvest lasts from the end of December thru early April, and the *kaya* field is burned in stages over a period of about a month beginning in early March, before new shoots appear. Over 20,000 bundles of 2-foot circumference are harvested, primarily by hand, using sickles. An experienced man can harvest 60-70 bundles a day. Until the mid-1950s, it took too much time to commute to and from the grasslands on the mountains, so temporary shelters where harvesters could stay for about 10 days were constructed of bamboo and *kaya*.

九州、沖縄の分棟造と高倉
Divided-Roof Houses and Raised Storehouses in Kyushu and Okinawa

平川家住宅屋根全景 (1988)
手前からうまや、釜屋、主屋が並ぶ分棟造

Overview of the Hirakawa House (1988)
This divided-ridge house has the stable, kitchen, and main house in a line (front to back).

竹の千木でつくられた棟
竹の根元が棟の妻飾りにあしらわれている
This ridge is made with bamboo *chigi*.
Bamboo roots decorate the ends of the ridge.

平川家住宅(国指定重要文化財　福岡県うきは市、2008)
右が主屋で左が釜屋
その主屋と釜屋を大きな軒樋でつなぎ、内部が一体化されている
The Hirakawa House (Important Cultural Property; Ukiha, Fukuoka Pref., 2008)
The main house is on the right, the kitchen on the left.
The two buildings are linked by a large trough under the eaves, unifying the interior.

分棟造

九州や沖縄地方の民家を特徴づけるものとして、分棟造がある。これは、主屋と離して釜屋(台所)を別棟とするつくりかたで、温暖な地域において、火を使うスペースをできるだけ主屋から離して暮らすことを選んだ生活の習慣に則したつくりである。また主屋と釜屋やうまやなどを小さく分けてつくることで、屋根を高く大きくつくらずにすむので、台風の多い地域で風による被害を少なくとどめることができる。北部九州では分棟造の主屋と釜屋が軒樋で内部が一体化された独自な発達形態を見ることができる。
この分棟造は本州の太平洋岸に沿って、静岡県や千葉県、茨城県まで、その分布が広がっている。

The Divided-Ridge Style

The divided-ridge style, a distinguishing feature of houses in Kyushu and Okinawa, has the kitchen, living quarters, and stable in separate structures, a practical arrangement in the warm climate. In addition, this enables the roofs to be kept low, minimizing typhoon wind damage. A unique feature in northern Kyushu is a trough under the eaves that unifies the main house and the kitchen.
Divided-ridge houses are also found along the Pacific coast in Shizuoka, Chiba, and Ibaraki prefectures.

平川家住宅正面
左からうまや、釜屋、主屋が軒を連ねて並ぶ
釜屋と主屋は後の増築で鍵形に一体化されている

Front view of the Hirakawa House
This divided-ridge house has the stable, the kitchen, and the main house built in a row (left to right).
The kitchen and the main house were added later, forming an L shape.

黒木家住宅（宮崎県高原町、現在は宮崎県立総合博物館に移築、2008）　左がオモテ（座敷）で右がナカエ（釜屋）

The Kuroki House (Takahara, Miyazaki Pref.; now moved to the Miyazaki Prefectural Museum of Nature and History, 2008)
The formal front room is on the left, the kitchen on the right.

オモテとナカエの間をつなぐテノマ

The space joining the front room and the kitchen

竹葺きの庇　真竹を二つ割りにして瓦のように庇を葺いてある

Pent roof covered with bamboo that has been split in half and used like tile

棟も竹簀巻で押さえる

The ridge, too, is held down with a bamboo wrapping.

南九州、沖縄の分棟造

南九州から沖縄諸島にかけては、分棟造の多様な発達が見られる。沖縄では主屋と釜屋が離れているのに対して、南九州では、主屋と釜屋が軒を接して下屋でつながれることが多い。南九州ではこれをナカエ造と呼ぶ。

主屋がオモテと呼ばれる座敷でナカエは釜屋であり一画に板張りの居間がある。それらがテノマ（樋の間）と呼ばれる下屋の庇でつながれる。オモテは開放的なつくりであるのに対して、ナカエは壁で囲われた閉鎖的なつくりであるところも特徴である。

また、鹿児島や奄美地方ではオモテとナカエに加えて、うまや、納屋などが3棟連なる茅葺きの分棟造の民家が独自の茅葺き屋根景観をつくり上げてきた。

Divided-Ridge Houses of Southern Kyushu and Okinawa

Many kinds of divided-ridge roofs have developed in the area from southern Kyushu through the Ryukyus. Whereas the main house and the kitchen are completely separated in Okinawa, in southern Kyushu the two structures are frequently built with their eaves adjoining and are unified with an extension between them. In southern Kyushu, a formal front room is followed by the kitchen, which includes a wooden-floored family room. These are linked by an extension. Characteristically, the front room is an open structure, but the kitchen is enclosed with a wall. In Kagoshima and the Amami region, a stable or barn make a third roof in the group, creating a unique landscape of divided-ridge thatched houses.

南西諸島の高倉
Raised Storehouses of the Ryukyus

鹿児島県奄美市（旧大和村）の群倉ボレ倉 (2008)
6棟の高倉が集落のはずれに群を成して建ち並ぶ

A group of storehouses in Amami (formerly Yamato village), Kagoshima Pref. (2008)
Six raised storehouses form this group at the edge of the village.

屋敷の一画に建つ高倉
（鹿児島県龍郷町、2002）

A raised storehouse in one corner of a private property
(Ryugo, Kagoshima Pref., 2002)

高倉の大きな庇の下は、農作業や憩いの場所として使われる

The large shaded space under the raised storehouse is used for farm tasks and resting.

南西諸島の高倉

奄美地方から沖縄諸島にかけて、高倉が広く分布している。高倉は正方形の平面で、4本足で支えられた急勾配の茅葺き屋根の屋根裏が穀倉となっており、床下からはしごで出入りする。この地方の高温多湿な気候の中で、厚く大きな茅葺き屋根で日差しを遮り、雨を除け、そして高床とすることで湿気を避け、またねずみなどの害を防ぎ、モミ、穀物を傷むことなく長期間保存するしくみである。

これらの地方では、毎年のように台風が襲来し、稲作をはじめとする穀物の生産が不安定で、数年に一度の凶作も避けられない。そのためにこの高倉での食料貯蔵は、生き延びるために必要不可欠なものであった。使用する木材も吟味され、堅牢で美しく、豊かな実りを祈る象徴として洗練されていった。

また、高倉の下は茅葺きの大きな庇に覆われて、高床の縁台として農作物の乾燥など農作業の場として使われ、また四阿として集落の人々の格好の交流の場でもあった。高倉は屋敷の一画につくられる場合もあるが、集落から離れた海岸に群倉ボレ倉として立地する場合もある。これは主屋が火災にあった場合にも、高倉がその被害を免れるためである。ボレ倉では秋に集落そろって収穫の作業が行われ、離島で暮らす村人の結び付きを表している。

高倉の笄棟（龍郷町、2002）
竹簀の子で巻いて、棟際の笄からとった縄でしっかりと結ぶ
The skewered ridge of a raised storehouse in Ryugo (2002)
It is covered with bamboo slats and firmly tied with ropes to skewers just below the ridge.

高倉の置千木棟（奄美市徳之島、2002）
徳之島の棟は千木で押さえられる
The ridge of a raised storehouse finished with *chigi* (Toku-no-Shima, Amami, 2002)
The roofs of Toku-no-Shima are held down with *chigi*.

Raised Storehouses of the Ryukyus

Raised storehouses are widely distributed from the Amami area to the Ryukyus. The raised storehouse has a square floorplan with a steep thatched roof supported by four posts. The roof space is for storing grain and is entered from under the floor by a ladder. In the hot, humid climate of this area, the large, thickly-thatched roof keeps out sun and rain, and the raised floor wards off damp and vermin, making it possible to preserve rice and other grain undamaged for a long time.

Because these regions are frequented by typhoons every year, production of rice and other grains is unstable, and a crop failure every few years is unavoidable. Because of this, storing grain in these storehouses was indispensable for survival, and the wood used was carefully selected for strength and beauty, a refined symbol of prayers for a bountiful harvest.

Under the storehouse, a large thatched pent roof enabled the space to be used as a porch for drying produce and for other farm tasks and also as a place where villagers could socialize. Raised storehouses were sometimes built on private property, but in some places they were built in groups along the shore, away from the village, to protect them in case of a house fire. Where storehouses were grouped like this, the entire village undertook the harvesting work together in the fall, a demonstration of the ties that bind villagers living on distant islands.

奄美の屋根葺き (2002)
足裏にワラ縄の草履を巻き付けて強く踏みしめて下地にしっかり縄でとめる

Thatching in Amami (2002)
The thatcher ties straw-rope zori to his soles and stomps hard on the thatch to secure it firmly to the frame.

奄美の高倉の葺き替えの風景（名瀬市）
View of thatching a raised storehouse in Naze, Amami

平葺き　足で踏み固めて縄をきつく縛る
Thatching the side
The thatch is stomped down hard and tied tightly with rope.

内部で上から針で差した縄を垂木にまわして外に戻す
Under the roof, the rope that has been pushed through the *kaya* with a needle is passed around a rafter and returned to the outside.

棟はほぼ円形におしぼこをまわして、棟茅を押さえる
To hold down the ridge thatch, sways are laid in a near circle around the ridge.

高倉の屋根下地
棟木に丸太の垂木を架け渡し、割竹をまわして下地をつくる
The roof frame of a raised storehouse
Round log rafters are laid across the ridgepole and split bamboo is laid around it to form the frame.

棒で茅束を上げる
Passing a bundle of *kaya* up the roof using a pole

奄美の茅葺き

奄美の茅葺き屋根は、ススキまたはチガヤで葺かれている。チガヤはススキに比べると丈も低く柔らかいので、風雨の厳しいこの地方で棟をしっかり包み雨を凌ぐ上で欠かせない材料であった。棟木に垂木を架け渡して、その上に割竹で下地をつくるが、隅は竹の下地で回して丸くおさめる。茅を葺く際にも、四隅をまわりながら葺き上げていく。茅が台風でめくられないように、しっかり縄で下地に固定するために、足を高く振り上げて叩き締める豪快な葺き方。足裏には、ワラ縄で巻いた巨大な草履のようなものを履いて、それで何度も茅を踏み固めるのである。

Thatch in Amami

Amami's roofs are thatched with *susuki* or *chigaya*. *Chigaya* is shorter and more pliant than *susuki*, making it an indispensable material for finishing the ridge to keep out the heavy rains that come to this region. The rafters are set against the ridgepole, and the roof frame is made over them with split bamboo, which is wrapped around the corners. *Kaya* is also laid on while rounding the corners. The method of thatching is dramatic, with the thatcher lifting his leg high to fasten the ropes firmly to the frame so the *kaya* does not get blown off by typhoon winds. The thatcher wears footgear of wound rice straw, like giant straw sandals, with which he stomps on the thatch many times to tighten it.

沖縄の竹葺き
Bamboo Thatch in Okinawa

沖縄の竹葺きの民家（沖縄県名護市、2002）

A house thatched with bamboo in Okinawa (Nago, Okinawa Pref., 2002)

ヤンバル竹を逆葺きとして、棟は竹簀で巻き笄に縄でしっかりくくり付ける

Thatch of indigenous bamboo is laid upside down; the ridge is covered with bamboo slats and tied firmly to skewers.

ヤンバル竹の茅束
A bundle of indigenous bamboo *kaya*

棟茅に使うチガヤ
Chigaya for the ridge

カミアサギ（沖縄県国頭村、2002）
沖縄の伝統的な祭祀の場

Kamiasagi (Kunigami, Okinawa Pref., 2002)
A place for traditional Okinawan religious ceremonies

竹葺きの屋根葺き
沖縄本島北部から愛知県犬山市リトルワールド博物館に移築復原（1981）
Thatching with bamboo
This house has been moved from the northern part of Okinawa island and restored at Inuyama Little World Museum of Man in Aichi Pref. (1981).

屋根葺き工程　Thatching procedure

カヤアギャー（茅を上げる人）
安波では本土に見られるような屋根面の足場をつくらず、はしごを使って葺く。はしごに数人が表向きに一列に腰掛け、頭越しに次々とリレーされて茅が上げられる

In Awa, scaffolding is not used and thatching is done from ladders. A number of people sit on the ladder facing outwards and relay the *kaya* over their heads to the top.

ヤーフチャー（茅を葺く人）　ヤーシミャー（茅を締め付ける人）
束になった茅をほどき、むらなく敷き並べ、竹を束ねてつくったウシブク（押鉾）で押さえ、垂木からとった縄で結び固定する。このとき強く締め付けるために、棟木からあらかじめロープをとり、それにぶらさがり高くジャンプし、全体重をかけてウシブクを踏み付ける。屋根は必ず反時計回りにぐるぐる回りながら葺き上げられる

The bundle of *kaya* is taken apart and laid evenly across the roof. Sways made by bundling bamboo are laid across and tied in place with ropes from the rafters. In order to tie the sways tightly, the thatcher hangs from a rope attached to the ridgepole and jumps high, using his whole weight to stomp down the sway. The roof is always thatched going around it counterclockwise.

ヤーサチャー（針を刺す人）
屋根裏に入り、針で縄を外に送り、内に戻す。次に外側でウシブクを強く踏み付けるのにあわせて、2人で体重をかけて縄を引き、茅を締め付ける。縄は稲ワラを直径約3cmに綯ったものを使う

A thatcher gets under the roof and uses the needle to thread the rope to the outside, then threads it back under the roof. Next, in time with stomping down the sway, two thatchers use their full weight to pull the rope tight and fasten the *kaya* securely. The rice-straw rope is 3cm. in diameter.

ヤークワサー（刈り揃える人）
棟まで葺き終わると、軒先から茅を刈り揃える。現在はハサミを使用するが、以前は鎌で刈り揃えていた。硬い竹を刈りそろえるのは相当な根気を必要とする仕事である

When the ridge is completed, the thatch is trimmed from the eaves to make it even. Today shears are used, but in the past the tough bamboo was trimmed with a sickle, a job that must have demanded considerable endurance.

棟のつくり方　How the ridge is made

平葺きおさめ
Finishing off the flat sides

最後の押鉾
The last sway

棟積み茅を積む
Piling up the ridge *kaya*

棟積み茅を縛る
Tying the ridge *kaya*

笄を刺す
Inserting skewers

みの茅を並べる
Laying "raincoat thatch"

竹簀を巻く
Covering with bamboo slats

棟が完成
The completed ridge

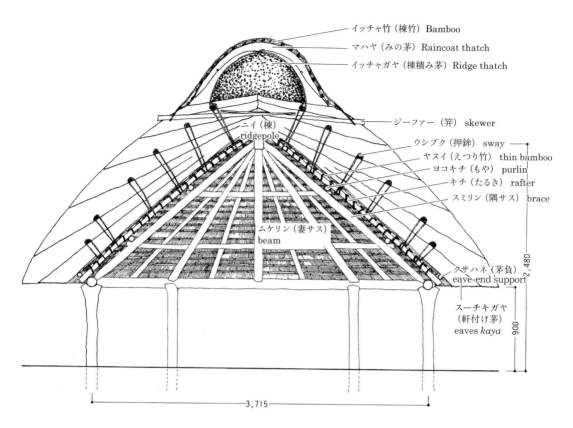

カミアサギ竹葺き断面図
Cross section of a *kamiasagi* thatched with bamboo

内部
Interior of a roof thatched with dwarf bamboo

沖縄の竹葺き

沖縄地方の茅葺きは、本島では笹葺き、先島諸島ではススキまたはチガヤで葺かれる。いずれも穂先を下に向ける逆葺きである。沖縄本島の北部では、ヤンバル竹（琉球竹）という細い竹が自生し、これを刈って屋根を葺いてきた。太さが1.5〜2cm、長さ3m程度の竹茅を軒付けだけは根元を下に向けた真葺きとし、そこから上は穂先を下に向けた逆葺きとして葺き上げる。台風の常襲する地域なので、縄でしっかり下地に結び付けるために、棟から縄をとって、高く飛び跳ねて両足で踏み固め、きつく締め上げる。こうしないと強い台風に屋根が飛ばされてしまうのである。

Dwarf-Bamboo Thatch Thatch in Okinawa

On Okinawa's main island, dwarf bamboo is used for thatching; in the lower Ryukyus, *susuki* and *chigaya* are used. An indigenous variety of thin bamboo, about 1.5~2 centimeters diameter and about 3 meters long, that grows in the northern area of the main island has been used for thatching there. On the eaves course, it is laid with the root down, but above that, it is laid on in reverse, with the tops facing down. To secure it firmly to the frame in the face of frequent typhoons, the ropes are attached to the ridgepole and the thatcher jumps high to stomp it tight with both feet and ties it tightly. Unless this is done, the roof will be blown away by strong typhoons.

竿棟のつくり方 (国頭村安波)
How Okinawa's Skewered Roofs are Made (Awa, Kunigami, Okinawa Pref.)

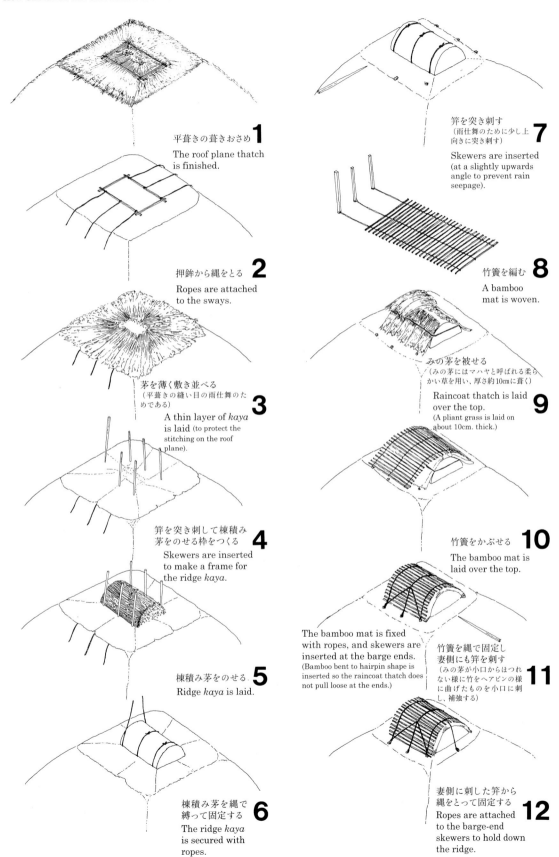

1 平葺きの葺きおさめ
The roof plane thatch is finished.

2 押鉾から縄をとる
Ropes are attached to the sways.

3 茅を薄く敷き並べる (平葺きの縫い目の雨仕舞のためである)
A thin layer of *kaya* is laid (to protect the stitching on the roof plane).

4 竿を突き刺して棟積み茅をのせる枠をつくる
Skewers are inserted to make a frame for the ridge *kaya*.

5 棟積み茅をのせる
Ridge *kaya* is laid.

6 棟積み茅を縄で縛って固定する
The ridge *kaya* is secured with ropes.

7 竿を突き刺す (雨仕舞のために少し上向きに突き刺す)
Skewers are inserted (at a slightly upwards angle to prevent rain seepage).

8 竹簀を編む
A bamboo mat is woven.

9 みの茅を被せる (みの茅にはマハヤと呼ばれる柔らかい草を用い、厚さ約10cmに葺く)
Raincoat thatch is laid over the top. (A pliant grass is laid on about 10cm. thick.)

10 竹簀をかぶせる
The bamboo mat is laid over the top.

11 竹簀を縄で固定し妻側にも竿を刺す (みの茅が小口からほつれない様に竹をヘアピンの様に曲げたものを小口に刺し、補強する)
The bamboo mat is fixed with ropes, and skewers are inserted at the barge ends. (Bamboo bent to hairpin shape is inserted so the raincoat thatch does not pull loose at the ends.)

12 妻側に刺した竿から縄をとって固定する
Ropes are attached to the barge-end skewers to hold down the ridge.

茅葺きの材料　Thatching Materials

ススキ　*Susuki*

日本全土の日当りのよい平地から山地に生息する。茎は根元から集まって株立ちして高さ1～2m。葉は長さ50～80cmと長い。花穂が8～10月に出て、尾花と呼ばれる。茎には綿状のものが詰まっている。茅葺きの材料として、普遍的で最もよく使われる。

学名　Miscanthus sinensis Anderss.

Grows throughout Japan from sunny plains into the mountains. The stems form clumps from the root, reaching a height of 1~2 meters. The leaves are 50~80 centimeters long. The ears appear between August and October. The stems have a cottony pith. *Susuki* is the most commonly used thatching material. *Miscanthus sinensis* Anderss.

カリヤス　*Kariyasu*

本州の東北南部から近畿北部までの日当りのよい標高の高い山地の草原に群生する。茎は株立ちし、高さ0.8～1.8m。葉は広線形で無毛。8～10月に軸からやや掌状に数本の花穂を出す。茎は細くて中空なので、水切れがよく、耐久性のある茅として珍重される。ススキをオオガヤ、カリヤスをコガヤと呼ぶことも多い。中部山岳地帯から北陸地方の多雪地帯で茅としてよく使われる。

学名　Miscanthus tinctorius, Miscanthus intermedius

Grows gregariously in sunny grasslands in the mountains of Honshu, from the southern part of Tohoku to the northern part of the Kinki area. The stems stand in clumps to a height of 0.8~1.8 meter. Between August and October, several ears appear in a fan shape. Because the stems are hollow, they shed water well, making it prized as a durable *kaya*. *Kariyasu* is frequently called *kogaya* ("little *kaya*") and *susuki*, *ogaya* ("large *kaya*"). It is frequently used as *kaya* in the area ranging from the mountains of central Japan through the snowy region of Hokuriku. *Miscanthus tinctorius* (Steud.) Hack.

オギ　*Ogi*

日本全土の水辺や池畔に生える。根茎が長く横にのび、茎は1本ずつ立っていてススキのように株立ちはしない。高さ1～2.5m。花穂の時期は9～10月で、ススキに似ているが色は銀白色を帯びる。茎は中空で硬くてしなるので、軒や隅などの補強に使われる。

学名　Miscanthus sacchariflorus (Maxim.) Benth.

Grows at the water's edge and on the banks of lakes. The root stems extend horizontally, and the stalks stand singly, unlike the clumped stands of *susuki*. It grows to a height of 1~2.5 meters. The ears appear from September thru October and resemble those of *susuki*, but are a silvery color. Having strong, hollow, flexible stems, *ogi* is used to reinforce eaves and corners. *Miscanthus sacchariflorus* (Maxim.) Benth.

葦（ヨシ）　*Yoshi* (Reed)

葦（アシ）は悪しに通じるのでその対語として善し（ヨシ）と呼ばれるようになった。日本全土の水辺に群生し、高さ1～3m。直径2cmにもなる太い根茎が地中を長くはう。8～10月に淡紫色から褐色の花穂が見られる。茎は中空で硬くてしなやか。茅として水切れがよく耐久性が高い。茅葺きの材料として、ススキに次いでよく用いられる。特に低湿地では、ヨシ葺きが多い。屋根葺き材のほかに古来よりヨシズ、スダレなどの材料としても使われる。

学名　Phragmites communis Trin.

Grows gregariously at the edge of bodies of water throughout Japan. The root stems, which may be as much as 2 centimeters in diameter, extend long distances underground. From August thru September, it puts out ears ranging in color from light purple to brown. The hollow stems are strong and flexible. As thatch, it sheds water well, making it very durable. After *susuki*, it is the second most commonly used thatching material and is frequently seen on roofs in wetland areas. It is also called *ashi*, but because this is a homonym for "bad," it is generally called *yoshi*, meaning "good." In addition to roof material, it has long been used for making mats, curtains, and other things. *Phragmites communis* Trin.

茅葺きの技
Techniques

シマガヤ　*Shimagaya*

シマガヤは霞ヶ浦周辺の茅の通称で、クサヨシ、カモノハシ、チゴザサが混ざったもの。高さ0.7〜1.6m。茎は細く中空でしなやかなので、上質な茅として霞ヶ浦周辺で用いられてきた。
学名　クサヨシ Phalaris arundinacea L.

Shimagaya is a generic term for the mixed grasses that grow in the area around Lake Kasumigaura, including reed, duckbill, dwarf bamboo, and several other varieties, when they are used for thatching. It can be found growing gregariously around bodies of water. It grows to a height of 0.7 to 1.6m. The stems are hollow and pliant, so it has been used for thatching in the Kasumigaura area, where it is considered a high-quality *kaya*. *Phalaris arundinacea* L.

チガヤ　*Chigaya*

日本全土の日当りのよい平地に群生し、高さ0.3〜0.8m。根茎は鱗片に覆われ、発達して深く地中を横にはう。花穂は4〜6月頃、長毛が多くて銀白色に光る。穂が若くて外に出ないうちに噛むとかすかな甘味があり、ツバナ（茅花）と称して子どもが食べる。南西諸島では茅としてよく使われる。
学名　Imperata cylindrical (L.)P.Beauv. var.major (Nees) C. E. Hubbard

Grows gregariously on sunny plateaus throughout Japan to a height of 0.3~0.8 meters. The root stems are covered with scales and develop horizontally deep in the ground. The ears appear from April through June, with many long, shiny, silvery hairs. When the grass is still young and the ears have not yet appeared, sometimes children eat them because they taste sweet when chewed. *Chigaya* is frequently used for thatch in the Ryukyus, with the heads hanging down. *Imperata cylindrical* (L.) P. Beauv. var. major (Nees) C. E. Hubbard.

クマ笹　*Kumazasa* (Bamboo grass)

北海道から西日本までの日本海側や四国や九州の山地にも生息し、高さ1m前後。このほかにも屋根に使われていたことから、ヤネフキザサという名の湿気の多い谷筋に生育するクマ笹の近縁種もある。北海道から日本海側の山間地で茅として使われる。葉先を下、外に向ける逆葺きとして使われることが多い。
学名　Sasa veitchii Rehder

Grows in the mountains along the Japan Sea from Hokkaido to western Japan, as well as in Shikoku and Kyushu, reaching a height of about 1 meter. A close relative that grows in damp valleys is called thatching *sasa* because it was used on roofs. *Kumazasa* is used as *kaya* from Hokkaido through the mountainous regions along the Japan Sea. It is frequently thatched in reverse, with the leaves pointing down. *Sasa veitchii* Rehder.

麦ワラ　Straw

成熟した麦の茎の乾燥したものを、麦ワラという。茎は細く中空でしなやか。屋根葺き材料としてはススキやヨシに比べると耐久性は劣るが、農業の副産物で、大量に入手できるので、戦後の食料増産時には平野部で普及した。一方、稲ワラは、麦ワラに比べると腐りやすいので、屋根に葺かれることはまれである。

The dried stems of mature wheat are used as thatch. The stems are thin, hollow, and pliant. As thatching material, straw is not as durable as *susuki* or reed, but its use as thatch spread through the plains in the post-war period, when it became plentiful as a byproduct of food production. Rice straw, on the other hand, deteriorates more quickly than wheat straw, so is rarely used for thatching.

茅葺きの道具　Thatching Tools

屋根に葺いた茅の根元を叩き揃える道具が雁木、茅を屋根の下地に縫いつけるのに使うのが針、葺いた茅の表面を刈りそろえるのがハサミ、この3つが道具の基本。

The 3 basic tools for thatching are the legget for dressing the root ends of the *kaya*, the thatcher's needle for stitching the *kaya* to the roof, and shears for trimming the *kaya* even.

ガンギ　Leggets

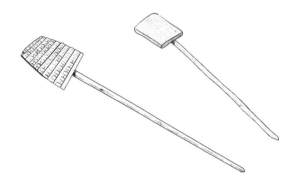

茅を叩きそろえる

材料はスギ、ケヤキなどを削って溝をつけた木材に柄をつける。溝のパターンと柄の長さと取り付け方向など樹種もかたちもさまざまで、職人が叩き揃え方や使う場所にあわせて自分に最適なものを自作する。
ガギ、ガギ棒、ガンギ、ツチ、タタキなど呼び名も地域によってさまざま。

Used to beat the surface into shape, these are made by carving grooves into pieces of split wood, such as cedar or zelkova, and attaching handles. The thatcher makes these himself: The pattern of the grooves, the length of the handle and how it is attached, and the shape and type of wood depend on how and where it will be used. The Japanese names for leggets vary with the region.

ハサミ　Shears

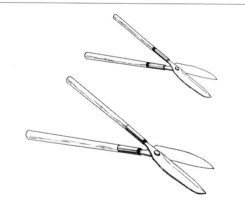

茅を刈り揃える

ハサミの刃が反っているのが屋根バサミの特徴。軒を刈るハサミ（コバサミ）と屋根の表面を刈るハサミ（オオバサミ）がある。ハサミの大きさ、反り方、交差部の形状などが地域によって異なる。

Used to trim the *kaya* to make it even. The curved blade is a characteristic of thatcher's shears. Small shears are used on the eaves, large ones on the roof plane. There are regional differences in the size and curvature of the blade and the shape of the joint.

ハリ　Thatching Needles

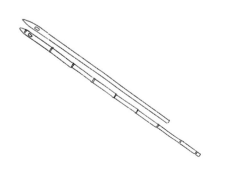

縄を下地に縫う

竹製、木製、金属製があり、直線状の針と釣り針状の針がある。縄を針に通して屋根裏まで突き通し、下地に結ぶ。

Used to stitch the rope to the roof frame. Needles may be made of bamboo, wood, or metal and be straight or hooked. Rope is threaded through the needle, pushed through the thatch, and attached to the roof frame.

茅葺きの技
Techniques

会津の道具
Aizu Thatchers' Tools

チュウバサミ　コバサミ
Medium-sized shears　Small shears

チュウバサミ　屋根の表面を刈る
Medium-sized shears for the roof plane

コバサミ　軒を刈る
Small shears for the eaves

カエルマタになった古いハサミ
Old shears shaped like a frog's legs

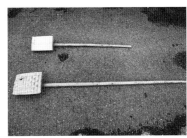

ガギ
Leggets

スギのガギ
Cedar legget

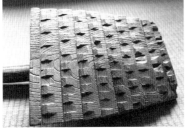

ケヤキのガギ
Zelkova legget

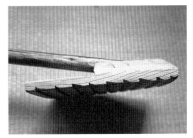

ケヤキのガギ
Zelkova legget

軒のナワトリ
Tool for threading rope on the eaves

カワヌイ　杉皮を縫う
Tool for stitching cedar bark

ナワキリ
Rope cutter

ナタ
Hatchet

オッタテボウ　差し茅の際、差し込んで茅を上げる
Pole that is inserted into the roof to lift *kaya* for making repairs

カヤヌキ
Pliers for pulling *kaya* out

茅葺きの棟仕舞 Ridge Finishings

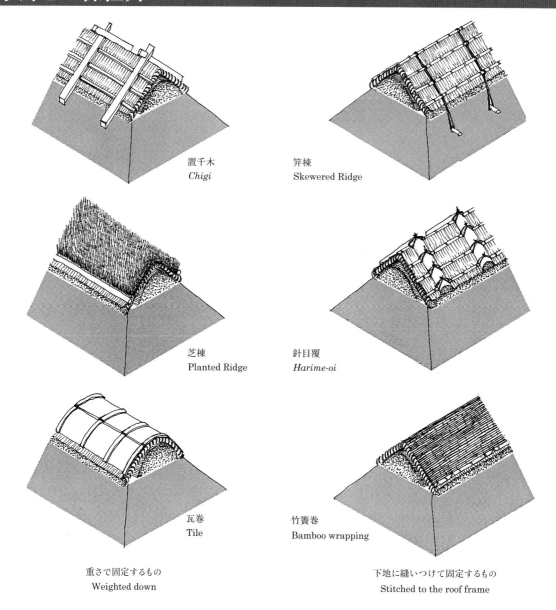

置千木 Chigi
竿棟 Skewered Ridge
芝棟 Planted Ridge
針目覆 Harime-oi
瓦巻 Tile
竹簀巻 Bamboo wrapping

重さで固定するもの
Weighted down

下地に縫いつけて固定するもの
Stitched to the roof frame

棟仕舞の分類

棟のつくり方、おさめ方を棟仕舞と呼ぶ。茅葺きは、茅を軒先から葺き重ねていき、棟で両側から葺き重ねた茅が交わると、その上にへの字に茅を折り曲げて被せる。これを棟茅またはみの茅といい、これによって棟の雨は外側に流れる。

そのみの茅を固定する方法によって、日本の茅葺き屋根の棟仕舞は6つに分類される。それは、棟を重さで押さえるものと、下地に縫い付けて固定するものの2つに大別される。重さで押さえるものは、木材をX字に組んだ千木を載せてみの茅を押さえる置千木と、土を載せてそこに芝を植え込んで土の重みと芝の根がからむことで押さえる芝棟、みの茅を瓦で巻いて押さえる瓦巻の3種類がある。下地に固定するものは、棟際に竿と呼ばれる棒を差して、そこから縄を取ってみの茅を固定する竿棟と、みの茅をおしぼに縫い付けて、その針目（縫い目）から雨が漏るのを防ぐためにそこに茅束をあててふさぐ針目覆と、みの茅を竹簀の子で巻いて押さえる竹簀巻の3種類がある。

Types of Ridge Finishing

Ridge finishing includes how the ridge is made and how it is held down and decorated. When the thatch laid on the planes of the roof meets at the ridge, *kaya* bent in an inverted V shape is laid across the top. Called "ridge thatch" or "raincoat thatch," it makes rain water drain to the outside.

Japanese thatched ridge finishings fall into two major groups: those that weigh the ridge down and those that are affixed by tying to the roof frame. Within these groups are six categories. Those weighing the ridge down include ridges finished by laying wooden *chigi* in an X shape over the top; ridges covered with sod and plants with intertwining roots; and ridges covered with tile. Those affixed to the roof frame include skewered roofs that have poles inserted for attaching ropes to secure the ridge thatch; those that have the thatch stitched to sways and the stitches covered with *kaya* to prevent rain from leaking down the ropes; and those covered with arrangements of split bamboo slats.

茅葺きの技
Techniques

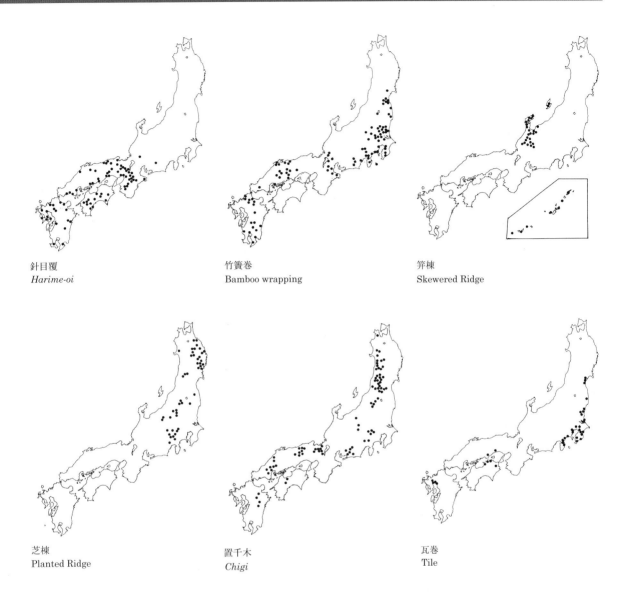

棟仕舞の分布

6種類の棟仕舞は、地域的な分布に特徴が見られる。まず、地域的に分布が顕著なものとして、針目覆は西南日本のみに分布し、芝棟は東北日本のみに分布する。この2つは、日本の東北、西南を二分してそれぞれ分かれて分布している。次に、全国的に広く分布するものとして、置千木と竹簀巻がある。しかしその地理的分布を詳しく見てみると、竹簀巻は西南日本から太平洋側の竹の自生する平野部の地域と重なることがわかる。一方、置千木は九州から東北までの山間地域に分布し、木材の資源が豊かな地域に重なることがわかる。それに対して、笄棟は北陸地方の一部と南九州から南西諸島にかけての2地域に限ってのみ分布する。これは、この2地域に強い文化的交流があったことによるものという説もあるが、この地域は共にユイで屋根を葺く習慣が続いており、ユイで葺く場合には素朴な技術である笄棟を用いた結果であると考えられる。瓦巻は比較的新しい技術であり、瓦の産地に近いところで用いられている。

Distribution of Ridge Finishings

The two types of ridge finishing having the clearest regional distribution are those having *kaya* stitched to sways and then having the stitches covered, which are found only in southwestern Japan, and the planted roofs, which are found only in the Tohoku region. Those most widely distributed throughout the country are *chigi* and bamboo slats. Close examination, however, reveals that the distribution of bamboo-slat ridge finishing coincides with the areas on the Pacific side of the country where bamboo grows on the plateaus. On the other hand, *chigi* are used from Kyushu to Tohoku in mountainous areas where wood is plentiful. In contrast, skewered roofs are found only in one part of the Hokuriku region and in the area from southern Kyushu through the Ryukyus. One theory has it that these two areas had strong cultural ties, but another postulates that because people in both areas thatched communally, the skewered ridge was adopted because of its simplicity. Tiling ridges is a relatively new technique found near tile-producing areas.

茅葺きの棟仕舞　Ridge Finishings

置千木　*Chigi*

くら型の千木
Saddle-shape

X型の千木・細棒を貫通させた接合
X-shape; joined with thin braces

X型の千木・相欠きの接合
X-shape; cross-lap joints

X型の千木・ほぞ差し鼻栓打ちの接合
X-shape; mortise and tenon joint with draw pin

垂直な端部
Vertical ends

直角な端部
Orthogonal ends

水平な端部
Horizontal ends

千木の形　*Chigi* Shapes

置千木

置千木はみの茅を横木で押さえ、その横木の上に木材をX字に組んだ千木をのせ、その重みでしっかり押さえる。この千木は棟に馬乗りにまたがるので、ウマノリとも呼ばれる。千木には、クリなどの水に強い耐久力のある丈夫な木材が用いられる。また、みの茅の上に杉皮を被せて棟の耐久性を高める場合も多い。千木の数は3、5、7、と奇数が用いられ、その千木の上に棟木が渡され、千木同士をしっかりとつなぎあわせる。その棟木の先端にカラスなどの鳥がとまるので、カラスオドシとも呼ばれる。

Chigi

For this, laths are laid across the roof to hold down the ridge *kaya*, then large logs are arranged in an X shape straddling them, securely weighting down the whole ridge. Chestnut and other strong, durable woods are used for *chigi*. In many cases, cedar bark is laid over the ridge *kaya* to improve durability. *Chigi* are used in odd numbered pairs, 3, 5, or 7, and are linked firmly by the ridgepole, which is laid over them. The end of the ridgepole is called the "crows' perch."

茅葺きの技 / Techniques

芝棟　*Shiba-mune* (Planted Ridge)

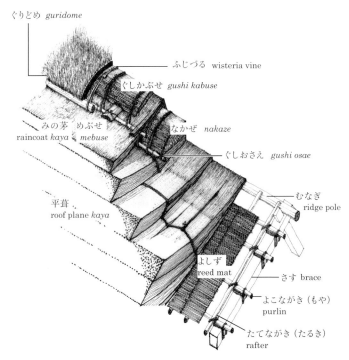

- ぐりどめ *guridome*
- ふじづる wisteria vine
- ぐしかぶせ *gushi kabuse*
- みの茅 raincoat *kaya*
- めぶせ *mebuse*
- なかぜ *nakaze*
- ぐしおさえ *gushi osae*
- 平葺 roof plane *kaya*
- むなぎ ridge pole
- よしず reed mat
- さす brace
- よこながき（もや） purlin
- たてながき（たるき） rafter

芝棟

みの茅の上に粘土質の土を厚くのせ、その上に芝を植え込んでその根を生やす。のせる土は、野芝を土がついたまま切り取ったものを、裏返しにして3枚ほど重ねて重しとする場合が多い。その上に同じく切り取った野芝を植え込み、その重みと根がからむことでみの茅をしっかり押さえるのである。この芝棟には、野芝のほかに、根が深く日照りに強い植物であるユリ科の多年草やニラなどを植え込み、さらにその根が張ることで棟が補強される。根が張れば芝は青々と茂り花が咲き誇る。その美しい風景が棟が丈夫なことの証しなのである。

Planted Ridge

Clayey soil is laid thickly over the ridge *kaya* and grass planted and rooted. The grassy sod for the roof is cut with the earth intact, and usually turned over and laid three layers deep. More grassy sod is laid on this, firmly holding the ridge thatch in place with weight and roots. In addition to the grass, perennial, sun-loving plants with deep roots, such as varieties of lilies and chives are planted, reinforcing the ridge with their roots. As the plants extend their roots, the grass gets green and the flowers bloom, creating a lovely sight and attesting to the health of the ridge.

茅葺きの棟仕舞　Ridge Finishings

瓦巻　Tiled Ridge

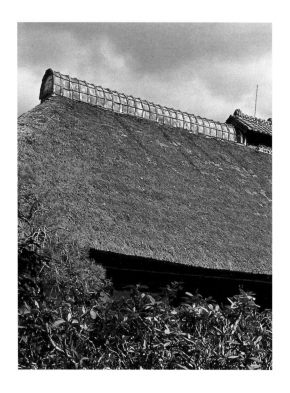

瓦巻
瓦巻は、みの茅の上に瓦を巻いて、その重みで棟を押さえるしくみである。瓦は、3枚又は5枚で巻く場合と、半円形の大きながんぶり瓦と呼ばれる瓦でおさめる二通りがある。3枚又は5枚で巻く場合には、その継ぎ目を漆喰でふさいで補強する場合もある。がんぶり瓦は、あらかじめ開けた穴に竹串を差して棟に固定する。農村に瓦が普及してからの比較的新しい棟仕舞である。

Tiled Ridge
Tile is laid over the ridge thatch to weight it down. This may be done by laying three rows of tile over the ridge, or by covering the entire ridge with a row of very large, single tiles. If three tiles are used, the places where they join may be plastered over to strengthen them. In the case of single tiles, they are affixed to the ridge with bamboo skewers inserted through holes made in them ahead of time. This is a relatively new way of finishing the ridge that spread after tiles became available in rural villages.

茅葺きの技 / Techniques

笄棟　Skewered Ridge

笄棟（こうがい）

笄とは、女性の髷（まげ）に横に挿して飾りとする道具のことである。その笄のように、棟際に横棒を差し込んで、そこから縄をとって棟に巻いてみの茅を固定するしくみである。笄を上向きに差すことで、そこから雨水が浸入するのを防ぎ、下地に縄を取らずにその笄から縄を取ることで、雨漏りを防ぐ。この笄棟は、下地に縄を取らずにすむので、みの茅だけを簡単に交換できるという利点がある。笄は両側から上向きに差す場合と、弓なりに曲がった一本の木材を山なりに貫通させて取り付ける場合の二通りがある。

Skewered Ridge

Logs are inserted through the thatch from the outside near the ridge and ropes drawn across the ridge are attached to these to hold down the ridge *kaya*. Inserting the poles on an upward angle prevents rain from seeping in along them, and tying the ridge ropes to the skewers rather than the roof frame also prevents leakage. This arrangement also has the advantage of making it easy to replace only the *kaya* on the ridge. In some cases, logs are inserted from both sides directed upwards, and in other cases a single curved log is passed through the roof so that the log curves upwards under the roof.

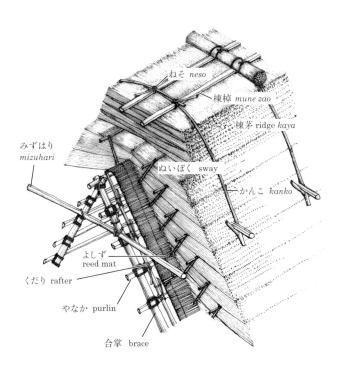

ねそ neso
棟棹 mune zao
棟茅 ridge kaya
みずはり mizuhari
ぬいぼく sway
かんこ kanko
よしず reed mat
くだり rafter
やなか purlin
合掌 brace

茅葺きの棟仕舞 Ridge Finishings

針目覆　*Harime-oi*

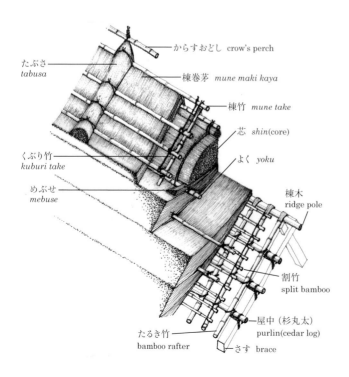

- からすおとし crow's perch
- たぶさ tabusa
- 棟巻茅 mune maki kaya
- 棟竹 mune take
- 芯 shin (core)
- くぶり竹 kuburi take
- よく yoku
- めぶせ mebuse
- 棟木 ridge pole
- 割竹 split bamboo
- 屋中（杉丸太）purlin (cedar log)
- たるき竹 bamboo rafter
- さす brace

針目覆

みの茅はおしぼこで押さえて下地に縫い付けて固定されるが、その針目（縫い目）から雨が漏り、また縄も腐りやすい。そこで、その針目に茅束でふたをして、雨漏りを防ぐしくみが針目覆である。その針目覆は、下地ではなく、おしぼこの針目ではない部分から縄を取るので、雨が内部に漏ることはない。しかし、この針目覆とそれをとめる縄は風雨にさらされて傷むので、そこだけ数年に一度交換して棟を維持する。
茅と竹と縄という茅葺きの基本的材料だけで棟をつくるという簡潔な方法なので、裸棟とも呼ばれる。

Harime-oi

When ridge thatch is simply held down with sways and tied to the frame, rain can leak in from the stitching and rot the ropes. Because of this, the stitched places are covered with bunches of *kaya* to prevent leakage. The ropes anchoring these bunches of *kaya* are tied to the sways in places that have not already been stitched, preventing rain from leaking into the house. This covering *kaya* and the ropes fastening it get damaged by exposure to the elements, so are replaced every few years. *Harime-oi* is a compact method of creating a ridge using just the basic materials, *kaya*, bamboo, and rope.

茅葺きの技 / Techniques

竹簀巻　Bamboo wrapping

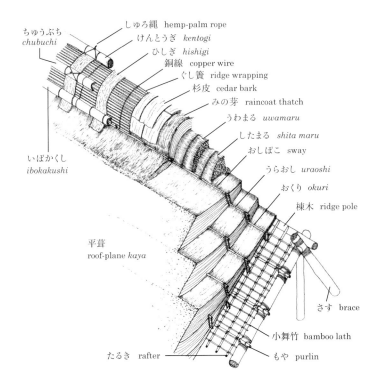

竹簀巻

みの茅をおしぼこで下地にしっかりと縫い付ける。その上で細い竹または割竹で編んだ簀の子でみの茅を巻き、その竹簀の両端でおしぼこにしっかりととめて固定する。さらに、おしぼこの縫い目を太い竹を2つ割にしたもので覆うことで、雨水の浸入と縄の劣化を防ぐ。また、みの茅を杉皮で被せてから竹簀で巻いて耐久性を高めたものもある。

Bamboo Wrapping

The ridge thatch is tied securely to the frame. Over this is wrapped a mat of thin or split bamboo, which is anchored securely to sways. The stitching on these sways is covered with the halves of a split bamboo to prevent water seepage and rope decay. To improve longevity, the ridge thatch is sometimes covered with cedar bark before wrapping with bamboo.

【編著者・訳者】

一般社団法人　日本茅葺き文化協会

茅葺きの文化と技術の継承と振興をはかることを目的として、2010年一般社団法人として発足。2018年国の文化財の選定保存技術団体に認定。毎年茅葺き民家集落を残す地域で茅葺きフォーラムを開催し、茅葺きの保存、継承に取り組む。

Japan Thatching Cultural Association

JTCA was launched as a general incorporated association in 2010. It holds annual forums in localities that still have thatched folk houses and works for the preservation and continuation of thatch. In 2018, JTCA was designated an Organization Supporting the Preservation of Selected Conservation Techniques for National Cultural Properties.

安藤　邦廣

日本茅葺き文化協会代表理事　筑波大学名誉教授　工学博士　1948年宮城県生まれ　九州芸術工科大学卒業　東京大学助手を経て、筑波大学教授、2013年定年退職　著書『茅葺きの民俗学』（はる書房、1983）『住まいの伝統技術』（建築資料研究社、1995）『小屋と倉』（建築資料研究社、2010）など

Kunihiro Ando
President, Japan Thatching Cultural Association

Kunihiro Ando was born in Miyagi Prefecture in 1948. After graduating from Kyushu Institute of Design, he became an assistant professor at the University of Tokyo, from which he received a doctorate in engineering. In 1982, he moved to the University of Tsukuba, retiring in 2013 as professor emeritus. He is a co-founder of Japan Thatching Cultural Association. His numerous publications include *Kayabuki no Minzokugaku* (A folklore study of thatch), Haru Shobo, 1983; *Sumai no Dento Gijutsu* (Traditional Japanese house-building techniques; co-authored), Kenchiku Shiryo Kenkyusha, 1995; *Koya to Kura* (Barns and storehouses in Japan), Kenchiku Shiryo Kenkyusha, 2010.

上野　弥智代

日本茅葺き文化協会事務局長　里山建築研究所　一級建築士　兵庫県生まれ　筑波大学芸術専門学群建築デザインコース卒業　筑波山麓にて里山を生かす住まいの設計に取り組み、茅葺き文化の継承と発展のための支援活動に取り組む

Yachiyo Ueno
General Secretary, Japan Thatching Cultural Association

Born in Hyogo Prefecture, she graduated from the University of Tsukuba, School of Art and Design, and is a registered architect first class. She is Director of Satoyama Architecture Labo, Inc. She is working to design wooden houses that utilize and preserve the environment of *satoyama* and is also involved in activities to support the continuation and development of thatching culture throughout Japan.

杉原　バーバラ

東京在住のフリーライター・翻訳者　日本茅葺文化協会正会員

Barbara Sugihara

Barbara Sugihara is a freelance writer and translator based in Tokyo. She is a member of Japan Thatching Cultural Association.

【参考文献】

『茅葺きの民俗学』安藤邦廣、はる書房、1983
Ando Kunihiro, *Kayabuki no Minzokugaku* (A folklore study of thatch), Tokyo, Haru Shobo, 1983

『住まいの伝統技術』安藤邦廣・乾尚彦・山下浩一、建築資料研究社、1995
Ando Kunihiro, Naohiko Inui, Koichi Yamashita, *Sumai no Dento Gijutsu* (Traditional Japanese house-building techniques), Tokyo, Kenchiku Shiryo Kenkyusha, 1995

日本茅葺き紀行
Exploring Japanese Thatch

2019年5月15日　第1刷発行
2021年9月30日　第2刷発行

編者　一般社団法人　日本茅葺き文化協会
著者　安藤　邦廣
　　　上野弥智代
訳者　杉原バーバラ

発行所　一般社団法人　農山漁村文化協会
　　　〒107-8668　東京都港区赤坂7丁目6−1
電話　03(3585)1142(営業)　03(3585)1144(編集)
FAX　03(3585)3668　　振替　00120-3-144478
URL　http://www.ruralnet.or.jp/

ISBN978-4-540-19116-9　　DTP製作／(株)農文協プロダクション
〈検印廃止〉　　　　　　　　印刷・製本／凸版印刷(株)
Ⓒ日本茅葺き文化協会・
　安藤邦廣・上野弥智代・　　　　定価はカバーに表示
　杉原バーバラ　2019
　Printed in Japan

乱丁・落丁本はお取り替えいたします。